GOTTFRIED BENN

MODERN GERMAN AUTHORS
TEXTS AND CONTEXTS

SERIES EDITOR: R. W. LAST

VOLUME SIX

GOTTFRIED BENN

THE UNRECONSTRUCTED EXPRESSIONIST

by

J. M. RITCHIE

OSWALD WOLFF
London

MODERN GERMAN AUTHORS—Texts and Contexts
ed. R. W. Last

ISBN 0 85496 046 5

© 1972 Oswald Wolff (Publishers) Limited,
London W1M 6DR

MADE AND PRINTED IN GREAT BRITAIN BY
THE GARDEN CITY PRESS LIMITED
LETCHWORTH, HERTFORDSHIRE
SG6 1JS

CONTENTS

ACKNOWLEDGEMENTS

Despite E. B. Ashton's excellent anthology *Primal Vision*, on which the present study draws heavily, Gottfried Benn still needs to be introduced to the English reading public. Although a vast amount has been written on him in German, there is still no book which gives a brief account of his life and works in English. This is what I have attempted to do, looking at the poetry and the prose from a critical point of view and making some attempt at explaining the significance of this twentieth-century writer to the non-specialist. Hence in the bibliography I largely ignore German critics, leaving the interested reader to find them in the specialist bibliographies which I list. Instead I focus attention on works in English which have proved valuable to me and which I hope will be a useful guide to further reading. I must record one special debt of gratitude to H. M. Ridley who allowed me to consult his excellent doctoral thesis for the vexed and intricate question of Benn's association with National Socialism. This thesis is a work which definitely deserves to be made available in published form to a wider public. I have also found the Australian scholar Marian Adams' *Gottfried Benn's Critique of Substance* most rewarding, especially after reading German philosophical and theological onslaughts on Benn's nihilism. Her approach to Benn's thinking is clear and precise and the parallels she draws between Benn and writers and artists from Novalis to modern times most illuminating. I have adopted some of her terms, for example, type-thinking and race-thinking, and followed her approach to Benn's primitivism, vitalism and formalism. Benn's background reading has been best traced by D. Wellershoff, who has also edited the works. Of the German critics the most helpful to me has been F. W. Wodtke whose *Gottfried Benn* in the Sammlung Metzler I have followed for Benn's life and works. But all Wodtke's excellent publications on aspects of Benn have contributed to this study.

Finally, I must acknowledge the inspiration which the critical writings and translations of Michael Hamburger have been both to me and also to Annabel Brown and Rick Kavanagh whose initials are given in the list of Sources of the Translations against the individual items they translated, and who bravely joined me in the brain-scarring adventure of attempting to express Benn in English. Like Hamburger I remain doubtful of the value of Benn's theories and critical pronouncements, but fascinated by the development of his poetry and the degree to which this 'seemingly hermetical work reflects a whole era of German, but particularly of Prussian, history'. The lines from 'Night Café' on p. 55 are taken from M. Hamburger and C. Middleton (eds.), *Modern German Poetry* 1910-1960, New York, 1962, p. 67; and the extract from Brecht's poem 'Of Poor B.B.' on p. 62 is taken from the same source, p.215; both translated by Michael Hamburger.

The publishers wish to thank Limes Verlag Max Niedermayer, Wiesbaden, and Verlag der Arche Peter Schifferli, Zürich, for using copyright material (cf. Sources of Translations and Select Bibliography).

8

MONOGRAPH

MONOGRAPH

Any selection from Benn's work will appear very
arbitrary and this little book is no exception. Readers
inspired to seek more Benn are recommended to read
Primal Vision, Selected Writings of Gottfried Benn ed.
E. B. Ashton. It is from Ashton that I have taken the
phrase 'unreconstructed Expressionist' to characterise
Benn, and if there is a difference between his view of
Benn and mine it is in the greater significance I attach
to Benn's Expressionism, though Ashton would not
fundamentally disapprove of my attempts to explore
Benn's life-long Expressionism. In fact this is what he
encourages critics to do.

By selecting poems from different periods I have
attempted to cover the full range of Benn's lyrical
output from 1912 to 1950. The prose presents a more
difficult problem, for Benn wrote many essays,
gave many lectures, speeches and broadcasts, wrote
various works of an autobiographical and semi-
autobiographical nature and various sketches and dramatic sequences. The limited selection here starts with
Ithaca, a sketch, and one of the Rönne stories from
his most explicitly Expressionist period. *The Address to
Heinrich Mann* of 1931 already foreshadows Benn's
troubles with the radical Left, while the notorious
Answer to the Literary Emigrés (1933) reveals the
depths of his embroilment with the radical Right. *The
Confession of Faith in Expressionism* (1933) shows
both Benn's attempts to come to terms with his roots

11

in that movement and his hopes that it could be reconciled with National Socialism. It is an important statement particularly in view of the current discussion over the extent to which he did or did not stay true to his Expressionist beginnings. The later prose is not represented here, but brief samples from the *Novel of the Phenotype*, *The Ptolomean* (1947), *World of Expression* (1949) and *Artists and Old Age* (1954) are contained in E. B. Ashton's *Primal Vision*. Even prose of this kind can be linked with Expressionist experiments in 'absolute prose' in the 1920's.

Gottfried Benn was born on 2 May 1886 in the village of Mansfeld. He was born in the house where his father and his father's father before him had been the Protestant parson. The Benn family tree could be traced back to the end of the seventeenth century and it was ironic indeed that he of all people should later be denounced as a Jew in the Nazi period. He had to prove that the name Benn had nothing to do with the Hebrew 'ben' (as in Ben Gurion) and was more akin to Ben Lomond or Wedgwood Benn. He was proud of his ancient (Wendish?) blood and strong Protestant heritage and liked to remember his childhood in the village of Sellin on the north German plain, where local lad and aristocrat could consort on equal footing. It was equally characteristic of Benn that he should be so scathing about the totally unartistic atmosphere of the family home in which there were 'no Gainsboroughs, no Chopin preludes, and a father who had only been to the theatre once in his life'. Like so many German poets he felt more drawn to his mother, especially perhaps because of her French-Swiss origins. His relationship with his father on the other hand developed into something more akin to the father-son conflict of the Expressionist generation. Benn was clearly given to race- and type-thinking and saw himself as a combination of the Germanic and Romance characteristics of his parents. The parallel with Thomas Mann's *Tonio Kröger* springs readily to mind, with the northern (Kröger) rôle being taken by the Protestant pastor father and the southern (Tonio) rôle by the French-Swiss mother.

Benn had his earliest schooling at home and then went away to school at Frankfurt an der Oder, where he found himself boarding with the son of a local aristocrat and a young man who was later to become a leading literary light in the hectic Berlin of the Twenties, Alfred Henschke (pseud. Klabund). Several of Benn's works are dedicated to him. Today, apart from his Chinese poems, Klabund is remembered only for his sensationally successful play *The Chalk Circle,* which became the source for Brecht's even more famous play *The Caucasian Chalk Circle*. The school was a good one and Benn was always grateful for the solid grounding he received there in Latin and Greek. Certainly the 'southernness' of the ancient world was to become one of the most important features of his poetry. Little is known of Benn's reading at this time, but the life and work of the German dramatist Hebbel seem to have made a deep impression on him. His lyrical portrait of Hebbel shows the extent to which he identified with the dramatist's lonely striving and suffering.

On completion of his grammar school education Benn went to the university of Marburg, where at his father's request he studied theology and philosophy. How much he gained from his two terms there other than a deep distaste for Kant is doubtful. However, he did begin to write poetry, modelling himself in part at least on Detlev von Liliencron, a soldier poet whose fresh impressionistic style had lately burst upon the literary scene. Perhaps Benn was also impressed by the completely unmetaphysical officer-and-gentleman rôle that Liliencron adopted in his works, especially in the collection called *Adjutantenritte*. There was certainly something about this man, who seemed so completely at home in the world of horses and women, that greatly appealed to Benn. Liliencron seemed to 'belong' in a way that Benn always envied but never attained. Officers, of course, should not write poetry. Liliencron overcame this difficulty by the unliterary *parlando* style of his poems, which seemed totally devoid of intellectual artistry and sophisticated techniques, but broke new ground for that very reason. In time Benn too was to make his mark with an equally unliterary jargon combining everyday slang, sporting terms, medical and scientific terminology etc., into a strangely artistic monologue capable of traversing all the forests of events from the beginnings of time to the first half of the twentieth century. Throughout, the slightly blasé officer tone was seldom lacking.

In 1904 Benn went from Marburg to Berlin. With few interruptions he was to be associated with this great city for the rest of his life. After a further year of study in the arts, he was at last able to transfer to medicine, when he was accepted as a scholarship boy for the Kaiser Wilhelm Academy. This magnificent establishment for training medical officers offered not only first class and up-to-date scientific facilities, but also general lectures on philosophy and art as well as training in the social graces required of an officer. Benn later summed up what he gained there as :

> Hardness in thinking, responsibility in passing judgment, precision in differentiating between the accidental and the fundamental, but above all that profound scepticism which makes for style.

Significantly, however, in such a materialistic-scientific context a great deal of his earliest medical studies were concerned with problems of psychology and psychiatry, the relationship between mind and body, problems which were to be central to his thinking for the rest of his life. When he graduated in 1912, completing his doctorate in the same year, he intended to become a psychiatrist, but found himself constitutionally incapable of dealing with mental disturbances. However, his training in problems of depersonalisation did find an immediate outlet in the stories which he began to write shortly after. Having had to give up a post as ship's doctor because of his proneness to sea-sickness he accepted a locum post as doctor in charge of a lung sanatorium near Bayreuth. A sanatorium was the setting for the story *Brains* (1915), with which the cycle of Rönne stories began.

Benn's earliest poetry shows the influence not only of Liliencron, but also of Rilke, Hofmannsthal and Stefan George. To that extent it was unoriginal and undistinguished. But he had also established contact with the new artistic and literary movement in Berlin : Expressionism. In March 1912, shortly after he graduated as a medical officer, Benn's first cycle of six poems was published by the Expressionist publisher A. R. Meyer, in a series of pamphlets which included the Italian Futurist Marinetti and the *erotomane* of

Expressionism, Heinrich Lautensack. Altogether this was rather a sensational start for a young officer and poet. These were no longer pale imitations, this was definitely an original voice, speaking of dead bodies, diseased organs, a decidedly big-city voice which went far beyond anything even the notoriously sordid Naturalists had ever dared to produce. Rilke, it was true, had also written a *Morgue* poem and Georg Heym had written a horrific tale called *The Autopsy*, so to a certain extent the themes were in the air. But with this short cycle of poems Benn was firmly launched among the new Berlin avant-garde and from now on his poems appeared regularly in Expressionist journals, in Franz Pfemfert's radical paper *Die Aktion*, in Herwarth Walden's *Der Sturm*, Paul Zech's *Neues Pathos*, René Schickele's *Weiße Blätter*, etc. Benn was admired by Carl Sternheim and modelled his theory of 'absolute prose' in part on Carl Einstein's novel *Bebuquin*. He gave public readings with Paul Boldt and Alfred Lichtenstein and, most important of all, became associated with Else Lasker-Schüler after her divorce from Herwarth Walden. His second volume of poems, *Sons* (1913), in which his poem 'The Young Hebbel' appeared, was dedicated to her.

In 1914 Benn published a little sketch *Ithaca* in the *Weiße Blätter*. This short dramatic sequence, which reads like a confrontation in the 1960's between young university radical idealists and a fossilised professor, already has the young interne Dr. Rönne as chief spokesman for the new generation against the old. Clearly the conflict is not only the typical Expressionist father-son conflict, but also a ferocious reaction against the step-by-step empiricism of modern science which refuses to draw any general conclusions about life, while life lived to the full, ecstasy rather than dull routine, was exactly what the young generation of the time wanted. *Ithaca*, the *parole magique* of the title and of the play's climax, conjures up all the dionysiac possibilities of the ancient world of myth to which the scientist Benn, disillusioned with the world of reason and logic, was to turn.

Benn, who suffered from a floating kidney, had early been invalided out of the army. The outbreak of war in 1914 meant his return to military life. By August 1914 he was a medical officer again and soon taking part in the invasion of Belgium, in which he won the Iron Cross, Second Class. By October his fighting days were over and he was posted to the occupied city of Brussels to take charge of an Army brothel. Here he lived a curious life in a requisitioned house, isolated, neither soldier nor civilian, without responsibilities or contacts, or knowledge of the language. This is the experience of life lived on the periphery of existence, 'where the collapse of reality comes, and the true awareness of the "I" begins' that he was to capture in the subsequent stories of the Rönne cycle. In the Belgian city Benn was deeply affected by the open hostility of the local populace, which only added to his personal disposition to alienation and isolation. However, his life in Brussels was not really so lonely as it was in his mind. He was involved in one great historical event there, when he had to attend as medical officer at the shooting of Nurse Edith Cavell. And he certainly did not lack for intellectual companionship. Carl Sternheim, the German-Jewish dramatist, whom he knew from his Berlin days, was already living in self-imposed exile in La Hulpe, near Brussels. And in the city itself he had close contacts with Otto Flake, Carl Einstein and Wilhelm Hausenstein. Benn rightly considered this period in Brussels as perhaps the most productive period he ever enjoyed. Not that he wrote much poetry. His third volume *Flesh: Collected Poetry* (1917) contained most of his pre-war poetry as well as the newer poems he had composed. There were not so many of these, but among them were some of his very best ever, 'Songs I and II', 'Caryatid', 'Oh Night' and 'Cocain'.

Probably more important than the poetry of this time were the prose works. The first of these, as has been mentioned, had already appeared separately in the *Weiße Blätter*. All the stories, *Brains*, *The Conquest*, *The Journey*, *The Island*, *The Birthday*, then appeared together in 1916 under the collective title *Brains* in an Expressionist series called *Der Jüngste Tag* which Franz Werfel edited. The prose sketches, *Home Front*, *The Surveyor*, *Karandasch*, which Benn also wrote at this time, were less successful, even on the level of parody, though hindsight does show them now to have been extreme foreshadowings of Dadaism, Surrealism and the Theatre of the Absurd.

Benn spent the last years of the war in Berlin. His first wife died, his step-son went to boarding school and his daughter went to Denmark to live with the Danish lady Benn met on the train coming back from his wife's funeral. The post-war period was not an easy time for a poet and by 1926 Benn was writing: 'Thirty-seven and all washed up, I'm writing nothing any more—it would be a matter of writing with tape-worms and filth. I don't read anything any more either—who is there?' However, autobiographical statements by Benn about how lonely and despairing he was must always be treated with suspicion. In fact, he *was* still writing both poetry and essays. He was engaged in various love affairs and even appeared in court as a medical witness in the sensational case of Wieland Herzfelde and Walter Mehring, whose Dada journal *Every Man his own Football* had run into trouble with the law over one of Mehring's anti-militaristic and obscene songs. His old friends Carl and Thea Sternheim, A. R. Meyer, Carl Einstein, Klabund, were all in Berlin. He became friends with Oskar Loerke and was involved in literary debates with J. R. Becher and E. E. Kisch who were already suspicious of his political inclinations. He gave talks on the radio, became a member of the Berlin PEN club, collaborated with Paul Hindemith on an oratorio, which was performed in 1931 under the direction of Otto Klemperer. All in all Benn became quite a prominent figure in the literary life of Berlin in the Roaring Twenties despite the image of himself as the lonely poet that he liked to project. In 1932 the final accolade of acceptance into the Establishment came when he was proposed for membership of the literary section of the Prussian Academy of Arts, an honour which Benn welcomed as the greatest which could be bestowed upon any German writer. Almost immediately, however, the Academy was riven by the political and racial tensions of the age. Benn's sympathies, despite his avant-garde background, were clearly with the nationalist-conservative against the radical-democratic wing. By February 1933 Heinrich Mann was making his attack on the National Socialist government which had come to power and very soon afterwards he and nearly all the respectable members of the academy had left or been forced out, to be replaced by the new wave of arch conservatives and purveyors of 'blood and soil'. It was at this point that Benn threw in his lot completely with the National Socialist movement.

Within about a year and a half he was totally disillusioned and could see quite clearly what the brown battalions meant for Germany and the world. But he never publicly retracted or openly attacked the National Socialist régime. He himself was soon under fire from certain quarters, but no more than any other avant-garde artists of the Expressionist generation who were denounced *in toto* as cultural Bolshevists, decadent Jews and corrupt big-city intellectuals. In the end when it became no longer possible for him either to publish or practise medicine, he did not leave the country, which would have been unthinkable after the scorn he had poured on 'liberal' emigrés before. Instead he took what he called 'the aristocratic form of emigration' by joining the army again as a medical officer. It was with the protection of the army, surely the safest place to be at this time, that he was able not only to survive the purges of the Nazi régime and the war years, but also to continue to think, write and even publish. His now became what he himself called a 'Double Life', split between normal reality and the life of the mind. The poems he produced became 'static', divorced from the world outside, sufficient unto themselves. It is impossible to feel overmuch sympathy with Benn when he complains how lonely and isolated he was throughout this period. There were too many who could not emigrate into the army, too many suffering unspeakable hardships in exile or concentration camp and death in extermination chamber. Benn's greatest hardship seems to have been that for some time he had to live in Hanover instead of Berlin. He was after all an officer in a position even to engage a private secretary whom he later married. And by 1937 he was allowed to return to Berlin and was even employed at the General High Command. His duties were routine administrative tasks which left him sufficient time for his own work. Apart from intermittent attacks from certain individuals, Benn seems never to have been in any danger from Nazi quarters. The danger he lived with was that shared by anybody living in Berlin at that time, namely air-raids. Towards the end of the war his office was evacuated to Landsberg, but his wife was able to accompany him. When the final collapse in the East came they both made their way back to the capital. Benn was an eye-witness of the struggle for Berlin, the destruction of the city and the last throes of the Third Reich. He survived everything. His wife, however, did not. He had sent her away to escape the street-fighting and the bombing. Tragically she poisoned herself in July 1945 apparently in desperation when she believed herself cut off by the Russians. Benn was alone once more in the now shattered city. By the end of the following year he had married for the third time. His new bride was a young dentist called Ilse Kaul, who moved her practice into his old flat. In his remarks on Rilke Benn singles out the famous phrase : 'Who speaks of victory?—survival is all!' For a twentieth-century poet this was to prove the most difficult art to learn. Most of Benn's contemporaries from the Expressionist generation were long dead. But survive he did. And he did more than merely survive the hardships of the war years and the post-war period of hardship and restrictions, he carried on his medical practice and wrote and wrote!

When the war was over, Benn was on everybody's black-list and attacked particularly for his National Socialist affiliations by other survivors from the Expressionist years, contemporaries like J. R. Becher and Alfred Döblin, who held important positions in East and West Germany respectively. But despite his past Benn was soon publishing again, capturing the public interest with a stream of works both old and new, poetry and prose, novels and pieces for radio. Generally his personality and his extreme intellectual position aroused as much interest as his poetry, especially when in autobiographical works like *The Way of an Intellectualist* with its new second section *Double Life* he again brought up the vexed question of National Socialism and how he personally had responded to it. Soon he was a controversial figure, much in demand for lectures and ceremonial occasions. In 1951 he gave his famous address on *Problems of Lyric Poetry* at the University of Marburg, which he repeated in French on 12 September 1952 at the Biennale Internationale de Poésie in Belgium. He was awarded the Georg Büchner Prize by the German Academy for Language and Literature in Darmstadt. His second major radio play *The Voice behind the Curtain* (1951) was broadcast and widely discussed. He was honoured by the Federal Republic; and right up to the last years of his life he seemed to be constantly travelling, giving lectures and public addresses. He was the most widely discussed literary figure in Germany in the post-war period and there is no doubt whatsoever that he enjoyed his 'comeback' immensely. He died on 7 July 1956 of cancer of the spine.

Benn's life was not an exceptional one, indeed some would argue that his life was more typical than exceptional, typical, that is, of certain intellectual and political developments in Germany between the wars. It has been claimed, for example, that German cultural life as a whole tended to lurch from one extreme to another at this time, and that the particular attitudes which Benn assumed both philosophically and aesthetically represented only typical swings of the pendulum. The 'swing of the pendulum' theory may be an obvious oversimplification, but it is a salutary reminder that there was a great deal of radical political and religious thinking then as well as Benn-type apolitical and nihilistic views. The truth of the matter is that Germany's course was so disjointed and complex that there was a crying need for radical panaceas. But then not only Germany, the whole of Western Europe had been following an extremely erratic course and an authority like Hugo Friedrich has been able to demonstrate quite easily that apocalyptic poetry of the type written by Benn is typical rather than unique and fits in extremely well with general developments favouring the abnormal, the absurd, the disorientated, and the rest. Alienation, dissonance, ugliness, incoherence, lack of realism : these terms commonly applied to Benn's poetry are thereby seen as features common to a particular strain of twentieth-century European poetry. This is not to say that all modern poetry is like this. As far as German poetry is concerned it is quite easy to demonstrate that there were still a great many poets who did not subscribe to views of universal

nihilism and continued to write traditional forms of
nature and religious poetry. Nevertheless such poets
were generally felt to be less 'modern' than poets like
Benn. It was Benn at least in Germany who seemed to
speak to the dilemma of modern urban man. The very
fact of his extreme philosophical position and his
esoteric and difficult utterances was what German
critics singled out as placing him in the vanguard of
'modern' poetry.

This is how Edgar Lohner, for instance, saw Benn.
For him Benn was not only one of the foremost
modern European lyric poets, but also one whose work
was open to comparison with that of such Anglo-
American lyric-reflective writers as T. S. Eliot, Ezra
Pound, W. H. Auden and Wallace Stevens. As a
footnote he added: 'With Eliot in scrupulousness of
style, with Pound in scope, with Auden in formal
invention and use of the vernacular, with Stevens in
content (ideas on the value of poetry and expression).'
Certainly this pinpoints important features of Benn's
work, scrupulous style, vast scope, linguistic and formalistic experiments, though on the whole non-
German readers of Benn have shown little interest in
his theoretical excursions on poetry. Generally speaking
it is only in the eyes of Germans and German scholars
that Benn is treated as a poet of international standing. Outside Germany in the English- and French-
speaking world his work is still too little known. While
German poets like Hölderlin and Rilke are now
readily available in excellent translations and the critical discussion of their European significance continues
apace, Benn's importance still remains largely
obscured. Many conflicting factors are involved in the
reception of any German poet in England or America,

politics naturally being among them. The fact remains that Benn has still failed to establish himself as a major figure abroad. Perhaps the lack of good translations of his work is partly to blame : he is often fiendishly difficult and his insistence on formal features of rhyme and rhythm make his poetry difficult to reproduce in another language without banality. However, even as early as the 1920's, Eugene Jolas had made the first attempt to introduce Benn to the English-speaking world through his journal *Transition*. But even these translations of Benn's magnificent early prose failed to produce any significant echo. Michael Hamburger's essay on Benn in *Reason and Energy* (1957) treated him seriously as a poet and gave some important samples of his work. Unfortunately Hamburger came to the conclusion that Benn was too restricted in tone to be described as a major writer. It was therefore not until the appearance of E. B. Ashton's *Primal Vision* in 1958 that a reasonable selection of Benn's prose and poetry was made available and a more general discussion of his significance could get under way. This book, however, was still rightly interested in the political rather than the poetic importance of Benn and though it gave a wide range of the essayistic writings, it did *not* include the lecture on *Problems of Modern Lyrical Poetry*. Since that date awareness of developments in *Modern German Poetry 1910–1960* has been considerably extended by the book under that title edited by Michael Hamburger and Christopher Middleton. While not focusing by any means on Benn, this anthology of verse translations has proved important for an appreciation of his work because it places the accent firmly on Expressionism. Most of the extensive introduction is devoted to a discussion of this movement 'since Expressionism initiated modern style in German poetry'. This should have been apparent since the 1920's when Eugene Jolas attempted to make the Expressionist poets known outside Germany and published an extraordinary number of their poems in *Transition*. Unfortunately his initiative was never taken up and these poets remained almost totally unknown until *Modern German Poetry 1910–1960* made excellent translations of key poems available in English in one attractive volume. For the first time this made it possible for the non-specialist to appreciate the richness of the remarkable generation of lyrical talent to which Benn belonged. Only since the appearance of this book have English and American readers begun to grasp Benn's historical significance. More and more he is being seen as a typical representative of a generation of poets that introduced Modernism to Germany.

Benn himself late in life pretended not to know what Expressionism was. Like all poets he did not like to think of himself as merely a part of a historical movement and preferred the image of himself as the heroic individual crying in the wilderness. And it is only fair to him to ask if he was in any way more than a representative of a comparatively obscure group of poets writing in a particular place at a particular time. Was there any feature of his life and work that marked him out as different from all his contemporaries? As has already been seen, he *was* different in one vital respect. He survived! He survived not only the First World War but also the Second World War as a more or less 'unreconstructed Expressionist'. Hence he was more than a poet who had played a controversial and sensational part in the hectic artistic

26

life of Germany in the Roaring Twenties when Modernism first came to that country, he was also even more of a literary phenomenon after the end of the Second World War. And far from being a mere antiquated survivor from a forgotten era of Expressionism, when he began to publish again after 1945 he seemed more relevant and up-to-date than anybody. Benn suddenly discovered that his lonely monologues were being listened to, his name was once again on everyone's lips. His essays were being read and his broadcasts discussed throughout Germany by people who would not normally have ventured into such deep intellectual water. Suddenly he was a 'fashionable' writer. The reasons for this kind of vogue often have nothing to do with questions of literary merit. In Benn's case the reasons for the sudden interest in his work were clearly often more political than aesthetic. One element stood out among all the others. Here was a poet and intellectual who had *not* left Germany when the National Socialists came to power. Not only had he *not* gone abroad, like so many Germans he had welcomed the National Socialist triumph in the warmest possible terms and had identified himself with the movement. Like so many others he had shared in the disappointment and then withdrawn into the private sphere. He had lived through the crucial German experience from beginning to end, unlike the exiles and emigrés, who, no matter how great and perceptive, could only comment on it from the outside. The German public was clearly fascinated by this man who had committed its own mistakes and who yet made no pretence that they had never happened. After the war Benn did not hesitate to include the 'incriminating' documents in a volume of his

27

essays, not forgetting the notorious *Answer to the Literary Emigrés* which he had composed in answer to Klaus Mann's strictures and which Goebbels had had widely broadcast.

Benn's *Way of an Intellectualist,* as he called the first part of his life story, was an answer in its own way to the question of how a thinker like Benn, trained as he was 'in that profound scepticism which makes for style', could possibly have been so unsceptical that he accepted all the false slogans of National Socialism. Here again his experience was not an individual but a typical German one. In another form the book was addressed to the question : how could the most cultured and highly educated nation of the twentieth century be so ready to abandon reason and accept such dangerous doctrines?

One answer to this question has been that it was the typical German feeling of not belonging that was to prove so disastrous on the individual and the national level. As far as Benn was concerned he was certainly a man who from an early age seemed personally inclined towards loneliness. It is true he made many friends, knew many women, had many affairs, indeed married three times, but always he insisted on his fundamental isolation. This 'outsider' syndrome was a national experience which on the political level only too readily developed into a pariah feeling for many Germans especially after the First World War. As a good Expressionist Benn treated this experience too in absolute terms and made his own personal (German) feeling of isolation into an expression of modern man's fundamental alienation from reality. That it was so much a German experience is shown by the form it takes in Thomas Mann's *Tonio Kröger.* In that famous story the artist is the outsider who longs for the normal middle-class world from which he is excluded by his artistic awareness. Benn too knew this longing for acceptance into a community. The artist-*Bürger* conflict so typical of Thomas Mann becomes in Gottfried Benn's Rönne a reflection of the extreme poles of the German experience of the Twenties, namely total alienation and isolation combined with a burning desire for community. Benn himself was always delighted by tokens of acceptance. So, for example, he gladly accepted election to the Academy and when shortly afterwards it was nearly destroyed by the political pressures of the time he did everything in his power to preserve the Academy even though this meant agreeing to the expulsion of certain individuals like Heinrich Mann, Käthe Kollwitz and all the Jewish members. The community came first, just as in Nazi ideology the Volk came before individuals.

Gottfried Benn never became a member of the party and never became involved in any atrocities. Some of his best friends were Jews. Perhaps his greatest 'crimes' were token events like his answer to the literary emigrés, allowing his name to be used, placing his signature on the declaration of allegiance to Hitler. Perhaps his greatest crime was sharing the general madness, going blind when everybody else went blind. There were, of course, varying degrees of blindness and perhaps it was foolish to have expected him not to go so blind so quickly. Benn himself would scarcely have admitted that he had been blind. Like so many of his contemporaries he saw no reason why he should do anything to stop the Nazis. It is well known that Benn's enthusiasm for National Socialism was all over within eighteen months and he was soon telling close

29

friends what he thought of the megalomaniac madmen who were governing his country. Yet this does not release Benn from blame, for it can well be argued that far from being a brief aberration in his life, the National Socialist phase was only the obvious political climax to much that he had always believed.

Even on such a key problem for National Socialism as race Benn's writings look very strange in the light of later developments. Of course, he could never be accused of anti-Semitism and he never advocated anything like the eventual elimination of so-called 'sub-human races'. However, like so many scientists and thinkers of his generation he did have theories of eugenics and breeding and as has been seen his whole thinking is imbued with 'the blood'. Like Ernst Jünger, Hanns Johst and other intellectuals of his time his whole *Weltanschauung* was fundamentally irrational. Throughout his medical and biological studies and after he constantly sought out theories and data that reinforced his belief in the basic falsity of reason and logic. In such attacks on the stultifying effects of nineteenth-century positivism Benn was by no means alone, indeed the fatal attraction of so-called irrational forces was a fairly widespread experience in both high- and low-brow circles in Germany in the Twenties. Attacking the scientific method did not mean that Benn or anyone else was thereby led inevitably into the National Socialist fold, but it was part of the general process whereby belief in man's ability to control his own destiny by economic and political means was ruinously undermined. Just as Sternheim attempted to undermine middle-class values by showing them up as mere protective covering over a jungle in which the survival of the fittest was the only rule,

30

so Benn too turned Darwinism inside out with his attack not only on any possibility of progress or evolution, but also on the whole of modern civilisation. Here again he found himself in good company among German intellectuals of a certain type. Spengler and others had made it almost a commonplace to set up the foreign and un-German concept of *Zivilisation* (something intrinsically artificial, rational and therefore to be condemned), as compared with the natural, national blood-ties of the *Volk* which provided the only true relationship between individual and community. This was, however, a dangerous doctrine, the possibilities of which the National Socialists were to exploit to the full when they destroyed all political parties but their own. Benn, like so many other alienated intellectuals, saw only the attractions of belonging to a national entity like the *Volk* and was dangerously blind to the dangers of appeals to the 'call of the blood'.

It is astonishing how large a part the blood plays in Benn's thinking. As has been seen, as a scientist he developed his own theories of eugenics and breeding, but even more revealing than such theories is the obvious appeal that the intellectual primitivism of the age held for him. Benn's primitivism was in fact typical of the modern intellectual's attempts to escape to a world out of time from the burden of 'history', which like Darwinism was generally despised as yet another accursed science invented by the nineteenth century. Intellectual primitivism, then, was one way of escaping from the alienating economic, political and technological complications of twentieth-century society into a simpler world in which man knew where he belonged. Drugs, alcohol, sex—all these are possible

31

means of arriving at the dream, the trance which frees the mind from the curse of thought and opens the way to a harmony attainable only somewhere out of this world. As Marian Adams has shown, it enriched Benn's poetry and prose 'with expanded perspectives in space and time, especially in the intensity of the response to remote and exotic land- and seascapes'. Primitivism assumes various guises in Benn's work, but however he varies the formulae he always comes back in the end to varieties of 'thinking with the blood' and appeals to 'low-level states of consciousness' as the key to the mysteries of life.

It was only a little step from high-brow longings for return to primitive communities to Nazi attempts to realise such longings with revivals of pre-Christian Germanic cults and barbaric ceremonies. It was also only a little step from another popular intellectual current of the time to Nazi practice. Life-philosophies were very much in the air in Germany from the turn of the century onwards and vitalism, as it has been called, was bound to appeal to Expressionists like Gottfried Benn. Again Marian Adams sums up its importance for him:

> It admitted unpredictability and an irrationally creative chaos. It thus provided an alternative to any deterministic scheme.

Benn could often be very scathing in his essays about theories of Life writ large, but in his own literary works the influence of vitalistic thinking can be seen from his earliest work on. In *Ithaca,* for example, Rönne complains that 'the totality of life' has been destroyed by thought and the playlet ends with a plea that souls may open wide to be fully receptive to the fullness and mystery of life: 'We must have dream.

* *

We must have ecstasy. Our cry is Dionysos and Ithaca.' But although this work ends with an explosion of violence when the student smashes the professor with his head, this does not mean that Benn himself was an advocate of violence in life. Unfortunately high-brow theories of vitalism such as his assumed a rather different character in the minds of the National Socialists and resulted not in irrationally 'creative chaos', but in the deaths of millions of people.

How blind was Gottfried Benn to the real implications of what he was writing? According to Karl Kraus it was by the failure of his relationship to language that Benn was led into political stupidity and guilt. Ridley sums up Kraus's argument as follows:

> Not only did Benn's hybrid language with its lack of discrimination against jargon and its rejection of grammatical connections between words, render him insensitive to the impoverishment of language by modern society: it also conditioned him to an acceptance of the shallowness and falseness of political slogans.

This is fair comment. Benn's montages and collages with words could on occasion produce startlingly effective poetry, but his language is indicative of a strong tendency to race- and type-thinking. To that extent he is yet another victim of general tendencies encouraged by the German language and its emotive words like *Blut* and *Volk*.

In his essay on Expressionism Benn claimed that he was a typical representative of a fundamentally apolitical generation, claimed indeed that intellectuals and artists in Germany from Goethe onwards had always been so. As far as his Expressionist colleagues were concerned he was being as blind and selective as usual because the movement as a whole tended to produce left-wing activists rather than right-wing conservatives. However, he did put his finger on a constant feature of the German *misère*, namely the alienation of the intellectual from political power. If the Expressionists as a whole were not apolitical, Benn and many of his fellow Germans certainly were, and being apolitical in Germany had always meant acceptance of conservative reactionary government. When the time for decision came in 1933 Benn saw no reason why parliamentary democracy should not be destroyed; he had never had any sympathy with political parties of any hue and he thought it quite right that they should be eliminated. Equally he saw nothing wrong with the muzzling of the press and the elimination of personal liberty. His own philosophy of the heroic individual brought him very close to similar Nazi beliefs in the heroic and made Marxist ideas of the subservience of the individual to the will of the masses particularly obnoxious to him. In this context it must be remembered how conscious everyone in Germany in the 1930's was of Marxism and dialectical materialism and Benn was no exception. To this extent therefore he was certainly not completely apolitical for he was extremely outspoken in his anti-Marxist views, especially regarding art and literature. Klaus Mann was therefore right in his tactful suggestion that it was dislike of left-wing radicalism which led Benn to welcome National Socialism as warmly as he did. As Ridley has summed it up: 'in avoidance of one horror he settled for another', and he goes on:

> Whatever else he may have seen in the events of 1933, the violent crushing of civilised democracy is certain to have appealed to him. Indeed he had been waiting for it for more than fifteen years.

Those readers who are familiar with Thomas Mann's earlier works, for example, *Reflections of a Non-political Man,* will not be unfamiliar with this particular cast of mind. Denunciations of the Treaty of Versailles, the Weimar Republic, liberalism, democratic principles, Marxism, and so forth, were unfortunately only too common in Germany. Even Heinrich Mann had been an Imperialist at one stage in his career, but had very early seen the error of his ways and developed into a leading socialist and democrat. Thomas Mann took a little longer to free himself from Schopenhauer, Nietzsche and Wagner, but in the end he too became a good democrat and only too well aware of the monstrosities which could result from distortions of fascinating German philosophies of irrationalism. Gottfried Benn never became a good democrat and never came round to seeing 'the error of his ways'. Consistent to the end he remained true to his belief that history was meaningless and absurd. The world in its evil course was simply staggering blindly from one catastrophe to another. Hence the meteoric rise and fall of Nazi fortunes neither surprised nor pleased him. He had welcomed their rise to power, been quickly disillusioned and then followed the typical German course of withdrawing into his private sphere. He never felt any need to act in order to bring about their downfall. He was prepared to let history follow its own blind course without any belief that what was to come would be in any way better than what had gone before. Such opting out proved a path many Germans were only too ready to follow in the post-war period. Indeed many Germans reading Benn's intellectual career could see their own dilemmas clearly reflected. Benn's thinking in the 1930's and after was

35

their thinking, his mistakes their mistakes—if indeed they were mistakes. The Benn problem was everybody's problem.

From all this it is clear that, despite his own often repeated theories of absolute art, Benn has rarely if ever been read for purely aesthetic reasons. This is not surprising for his poetry was rarely absolute and his essays never. In fact his work constantly forces the reader to confront the problem of ideology and art. He is after all a reflective poet like Eliot, Pound and Yeats, all of whom have at various times raised similar obstacles to appreciation. What is the reader's proper approach to the work of a poet of whose religious, political and philosophical ideas he strongly disapproves? None of the poets named raise the issue as clearly as Benn, for none of them was associated with a political movement so brutally mindless as National Socialism. Certainly in Germany Benn was the only poet who raised such issues. By war, exile and early death most poets of the Expressionist generation had avoided contamination with National Socialism. Rilke had died in 1926, Hofmannsthal in 1929, and Stefan George, who looked exploitable for National Socialist purposes, had denounced all it stood for before leaving Germany and dying in Switzerland. Weinheber, the only poet of any standing to be closely associated with National Socialism and an even greater exponent of formalistic gymnastics than Gottfried Benn, was an intellectual midget by comparison with him.

What made the ideological conflict so acute was the presence of Brecht in Berlin. In effect the battles of the thirties between nihilism and dialectical materialism were still being fought in the fifties round the figures of Benn and Brecht. These two men seemed a

36

key to the mentality of a divided Germany, and reading them together showed not only how far apart they were both ideologically and aesthetically, but also how close they were in so many respects. Both were highly intellectual and sophisticated writers reacting to the same set of circumstances—1914–18, the Roaring Twenties, inflation, the rise of National Socialism, the war and the post-war era of restoration. Against this background their works seemed complementary, indeed symbolic of the choices facing Germany. Similarities between Benn and Brecht were, of course, not always immediately apparent for both produced highly individual theories and critical terminology which were often greater barriers than they were aids to comprehension. However, similarities there were, not least in their mutual obsession with the problem of alienation. Brecht, of course, is famous for his simple poetry and use of popular art forms, while Benn is notorious for his formalism and linguistic obscurity. Yet they meet in their shared fondness for colloquial speech and aphoristic conciseness and precision. Both share the Expressionist generation's fascination with all things Chinese and in their poetry constantly strive after Chinese simplicity and wisdom. And with both poets it is impossible to remain unaware of the basic philosophy which informs their poetry. Benn's nihilism is as inescapable as Brecht's dialectical materialism. Yet is the validity of their poetry thereby destroyed? Is poetry didactic when the message is communism, but not didactic when the message is nihilism?

Benn and Brecht both had their spells in the wilderness before being rediscovered by a new public after the war. After a first period of fame and notoriety in the Roaring Twenties both had dropped into

37

comparative obscurity during the dangerous thirties, before surfacing again in the post-war forties. Both were survivors from an earlier age who had been closely associated with Berlin and seemed to belong there. Both were big-city poets, far removed from sentimental clichés of nature poetry. Their respective positions in the divided city, Brecht in the communist East and Benn in the 'democratic' West, assumed symbolic significance. There was something clearly ironic about the difficulties which a committed political poet had with doctrinaire Stalinism in the East, while neo-Nazis and new Democrats were fighting over Benn in the West. In this atmosphere no poet was immune from ideological exploitation.

While Brecht was making his little theatre on the Schiffbauerdamm into the most famous in the world, Benn's slim volumes of prose and poetry were preparing his 'reluctant' return to the lime-light :

> If for the past fifteen years like me you have been called a pig by the Nazis, a swine by the Communists, a spiritual prostitute by the democrats, a renegade by the emigrés and a pathological nihilist by the religious, then you are a little careful about stepping before the public gaze again.

But he was not really so reluctant. He had always been a sensationally provocative poet and essayist and there is no doubt that he enjoyed what he himself called his 'come-back'. The war that raged over him was lively in the extreme, for he fascinated his new public as much by the 'unspeakable' things he said as by the manner in which he said them. In post-war Germany he became a literary phenomenon of the first order, though non-German commentators generally showed little interest in his theories of absolute art and resolutely focused attention on the statements of Benn the anti-democrat in the thirties.

Benn's sudden popularity in Germany remains hard to explain. Ideological misinterpretations were responsible for some of it, both from anti-Nazi and neo-Nazi quarters. The sheer brilliance of Benn's formulations also impressed after so many years of Nazi double-talk and party political slogans. And like Brecht he still evoked nostalgic echoes of the hectic days of Berlin in the Roaring Twenties before the *Gleichschaltung*. But when all is said and done, Benn was clearly also striking wider echoes in a responsive audience. He was relevant to the post-war condition, he was the crystallisation point of many divergent tendencies in the cultural life of post-war Germany at the so-called *Nullpunkt*. Needless to say, this concept of the 'Zero-point' has given rise to a great deal of discussion. Rodney Livingstone has summed up what it implies in these words :

> The complete destruction of Germany, the apparent end of a tradition, the younger generation with its complete mistrust of its elders, i.e. not only political, economic and social convulsions, but also literary changes, the turning away from the Nazi prescription, the adoption of techniques from foreign writers like Sartre, Hemingway, Dos Passos, rather than from the German classics, the failure of writers (who like Wiechert and Carossa persist in traditional paths) to keep pace with the *Zeitgeist,* as well as of those who, having been abroad until after 1945, have missed the decisive German experiences.

Benn had not been abroad and had been a very good witness of the decisive German experiences. He had conjured up visions of the catastrophic upheavals before the event and had remained a cool observer of them when they came. He was very much in tune with the *Zeitgeist* of a post-war Germany which had seen all the traditional standards of the past totally destroyed. Indeed, having aided in their destruction he had long since faced up to the problem of 'nihilism and after'. Nihilism, which for so long had been the more or less private concern of post-Nietzschean intellectuals like Benn, had suddenly become a matter of public experience. So once again Benn was the phenotype of the hour. What he had been mulling over and refining for twenty or thirty years in highly sophisticated poetic and essayistic form suddenly struck a common chord. His radical nihilism suddenly struck upon the *ohne mich* disillusionment of the post-war generation in Germany with the force of a revelation. It was because he was expressing the common German experience that the 'difficult' poet with the austere cult of formalism and absolute art suddenly found that his lonely monologues addressed to no one were being listened to by a new generation which had grown up during the war. Not only did these people listen to him and apparently grasp some of what he was saying, they were very soon indulging in the highest form of literary praise, namely imitation. One of the features of post-war German poetry is the Benn school of poets. This was a miracle at which Benn never ceased to wonder, yet it is perhaps no more remarkable than the equally sudden vogue of existentialism, which from being a rather obscure and difficult philosophy suddenly swept into almost all art forms. The time was simply ripe for it. Needless to say, the spiritual climate in England and America after the war was not the same as in Germany. There was no similar 'Benn-wave' in these countries. There his time has still to come.

If Benn remains comparatively unknown outside Germany there is little doubt inside that country of the solid basis on which his reputation rests. For German critics he is simply a great poet and not merely one who at various times in his career has been in tune with the *Zeitgeist*. As a scientist he was a professional, always proud of his ability to keep up-to-date with the latest literature on his special fields of venereology, medical statistics, and so forth, and a regular contributor to learned journals. But his abilities in this sphere would never have roused much general interest and outside it he always showed a most un-scientific tendency towards selective use of data and unverifiable generalisation. As a philosopher and aes-thetician he was obsessed with matter and substance and never got very far beyond Nietzsche, from whom he quotes the same few central concepts over and over again. He is simply a poet—with an unconquerable urge to expression. Now that all his work has been published from the earliest writings of before the First World War right through to the 1950's it is possible to follow the changing forms this unceasing will to ex-pression took over the years. The critical question that remains to be resolved about Benn is whether he will be remembered for the poetry of the twenties which first launched him on the path to fame and notoriety or for the later works of the thirties and forties. On the whole, German critics immediately after the Second World War tended to favour the smoother and quieter Benn of the later years rather than the more violent forms of his Expressionist years. The *Morgue* cycle has still found very few friends. However, Benn is being seen more and more in the context of the Expressionist generation to which he originally belonged and even the 'static' later poems are now recognised as part of the same basic strain. Benn remained an 'unreconstructed Expressionist'.

What must be remembered is that Benn's first readers after the Second World War had little knowledge of Expressionism. They responded to his dazzling technique and cosmic visions with little awareness of his Expressionist roots. Only gradually did they realise that Benn was only one representative of a great literary and artistic movement which the Nazis had eliminated as decadent art. In time Expressionism has been exhumed and subjected to critical reappraisal, so much so indeed that it is no exaggeration to speak of an Expressionist Revival. In turn this has meant that critical evaluations of Benn's poetry have moved out of the polemical sphere of the immediate post-war years and their ideological conflicts. More and more it has been possible to place him in his historical context as the works of his contemporaries have become readily available again. Else Lasker-Schüler, who had been so close to Benn at one time, died in Palestine, but her scattered works have now been collected and published. Carl Sternheim, whose staccato, distorted syntax puts its mark on all his contemporaries, has been magnificently edited by Professor Emrich and his comedies are again being performed in every major city in Germany. Benn is no longer the sole survivor from a generation of poets. Indeed in literary reputation he may already have been overtaken by Georg Trakl, who from being a comparatively obscure minor poet known from a handful of poems in various anthologies has now advanced to the supreme accolade of a complete critical-historical edition of hitherto unsurpassed precision and detail. For a German poet this is an almost unheard-of honour of a kind which only Hölderlin has been afforded in modern times. Trakl's dark, chaotic visions of evil, decay and destruction have set the modern interpreter problems as stimulating and exasperating as those set by Kafka's hermetic prose. But despite discrepancies of interpretation there is no doubt about the value of Trakl's work which is also gradually becoming known even in English as more and more of it is translated. Benn, Trakl, Lasker-Schüler, Heym and one or two others: these are the poets of the Expressionist generation who seem most relevant to the present day. In this company Benn stands out first and foremost by the fact that he survived both the First World War and the Second. And he not only survived, he kept writing, producing work of a consistently high standard, making himself both by the volume and quality of his oeuvre perhaps the greatest lyrical poet out of a generation of poets.

One of Benn's very earliest pieces was called *Conversation (Gespräch)*. Some of his early poems, e.g. 'Man and Woman go through the Cancer Ward', are conversation pieces too, but he very soon became the poet of the lonely monologue. The dialogue form is, however, one link between this first stage of his literary career and his last. In the productive Brussels period, for example, he was inspired to write *Ithaca* (1914), *Home Front* (1915), *The Surveyor* (1916) and *Karandasch* (1917). Then late in life he returned to the dialogue with *Three Old Men* (1948) and *The Voice behind the Curtain* (1951). At no time can he be said to have been a great dramatic talent, but it was a form he found useful to express violently oppos-

43

ing concepts and ideas. This is noticeable already in the earliest of them all, *Ithaca*. The setting, as so often with the early Benn, is medical, indeed pathological. The focus for discussion is the brain, or to be more exact the cervical cortex. The professor's first speech is a *reductio ad absurdum* of a scientific method which leaves everyone concerned still a long way away from any understanding of 'the vast complex of forces which control the universe'. Science refuses to draw conclusions, leaving the theologians and mystics to do that. But what Rönne and the medical students really react violently against is the insistence on regulating experimental conditions and destroying the simple self-contained naïveté of things as they are, the individual case! They reject the mere collecting and systematising of knowledge as a puerile activity, they reject the positivistic hunt for data as meaningless fact-grubbing and pour ridicule even on the practical and humane arguments in favour of medical science. For what is the use of saving or prolonging a life, if life is trivial? Mortality is part of life and it may make life lose its value to take away death's sting. Once perhaps science may have served a useful purpose when it reinforced the belief in God, but now it serves only to destroy all faith. As Rönne himself puts it, thinking and logic mean the destruction of the universe. All that they leave is 'words and the brain'. This is the cross he is nailed to: the brain! God and the natural world have been destroyed by thought. The future holds far less hopeful prospects than those promised by the scientists. Mankind will turn into robots and computers capable only of systematising and classifying. This is not progress. 'The whole history of evolution is useless. The brain is a blind alley. A bluff to fool the middle

classes.' The experience to which Rönne and his contemporaries is giving expression is the classic twentieth-
century loss of centre ('Verlust der Mitte'), and these
are the very words he uses : 'What centre is there for us
to gather round?' Yet the possible means of escape from
the affliction of thought are also adumbrated. One is the
Romantic path of inwardness, turning in upon oneself
to where strange associations are found and mysterious
processes take place. Another is the path of regression to
a primeval harmony :

> Oh, if only I could return to being a grassy field, sand
> dotted with flowers, a vast meadow. With the earth bearing
> everything to one on waves that are warm or cool. No
> more brain. A state of being lived.

This primal vision of a return to paradise is expressed
by Rönne the doctor as a kind of Expressionistic *Mensch-
heitsdämmerung*, that is, the end of one world and
the dawn of another. The mystic voyage home has distinct echoes of Novalis.

The man of intellect is a modern phenomenon who
must be overcome by something more primitive. So
the new dawn will also see the appearance of a 'New
Man'. Paradoxically, however, the new man will be
old : 'We are the blood; from the warm seas, the
mothers who gave birth to life.'

The professor's new man, the *homo faber* techno-
logist of the twentieth century, is rejected in favour of
the man of blood. Perhaps in view of later developments in Germany, rejection of logic in favour of
blood may strike the modern reader as ominous,
especially in view of the violence of the play's language
and the physical excesses with which it ends. But the
juxtaposition of violent and poetic imagery was yet

45

another feature of the Expressionistic style and there is no suggestion that this scream from the heart is to be translated into real terms. Certainly there is no proto-Nazi Germanic madness involved, on the contrary the conclusion of the play with its Utopian vision of Ithaca is an explicit appeal to the Mediterranean and the South as the source of all that is most humane in the world. If the play is prophetic at all, then is it in the sense that the apolitical students who are led astray by this vision of the ideal south will in turn be destroyed by the brutal north? 'You callow youths! You murky dawn! Your life blood will be shed and the mob will feast in triumph over it.'

For such an early work *Ithaca* shows a remarkable number of elements, which were to remain constant throughout Benn's later work. But the real key seems to lie in the words: 'And once the mists had cleared what was left? Words and the brain.' There are always obscurities and difficulties in Benn's thinking, but these are the central concepts to which he always returns. This is true too of the prose work *Brains* which he was writing at this time. In this story Rönne, the young doctor of *Ithaca,* has left the pathological institute. Significantly he is travelling from South to North to take a locum post. He is suffering from a strange mental apathy brought on by performing too many autopsies. As he travels along he ponders the problem of reality. How can it be captured? One method is to write everything down in a notebook (the literary method of the naturalists). At first, however, the prose style of the story seems impressionistic rather than naturalistic: 'men out working in the hay/ wooden bridges/stone bridges/a town/and a car/on the mountainside/in front of a house'. But Rönne seems incapable of coping with this flood of data pouring in on him. He is lonely, distant, cool—but not with the detachment of the doctor. He cannot help analysing, breaking down even the simplest actions. Unwittingly the brain atomises reality and Rönne attempts to counter this process by mastering the world with words. Everywhere he looks 'words are a condition of life'. But the brain has lost its control :

> There is nothing solid behind my eyes any more. On all sides space surges off into infinity; once surely it flowed together at one spot. The cortex that was holding me up had crumbled.

It is not long before his collapse is complete. The loss of centre in this case is also a process of depersonalisation or alienation, but not in the Brechtian sense whereby the individual in capitalistic society is inevitably divorced from the real forces which govern his life. Here alienation is an extreme mental state of the kind which fascinated the Expressionists (cf. Heym's story *The Madman*). Madness no longer needed to be viewed negatively, it could also offer liberation from the affliction of the brain. And indeed this particular story ends as does Heym's with a vision of flying like a great bird. Benn later summed up the positive aspects of alienation in *The Way of an Intellectualist* in which he refers to Rönne.

> A kind of inner concentration began, a stirring of secret spheres; and individuality faded, and a primal stratum emerged, intoxicated, image-laden, Pan-like.

The Address to Heinrich Mann (1931) has been selected for inclusion here only partly because of its political implications. Benn simply ignores those aspects of his literary hero which he dislikes, namely the

47

Heinrich Mann who was also a politically active, Voltaire-like man of letters, politician and democrat. Instead he focuses his attention on Heinrich Mann the Francophile and develops round him, Flaubert, Stefan George and Nietzsche a highly idiosyncratic view of *Artistik* (artistry). This gives an excellent insight into what to expect from Gottfried Benn's own pen, namely *not* didactic poetry with humanistic ideals, but something reminiscent of art for art's sake, combining:

> From the west, intellect: fanaticism of expression, analytical instinct, versed in harmonies and as penetrating as X-rays; from the north the eruptive quality of enormous themes, the dark tragic dreams.

Already Benn was working towards theories of absolute art very much akin to the theories of absolute poetry he developed in his famous lecture on *Problems of Lyrical Poetry* at Marburg. However, theories of 'art without moral force' were to look quite different by 1933 when Benn was sending his *Answer to the Literary Emigrés* to explain how his reverence for literary figures like Heinrich Mann was compatible with acceptance of the new régime. Klaus Mann proved right in the end. Benn *was* an intellectual, 'the peculiarity of whose radical sense of language' earned him nothing but jeers and sneers from the Nazis. Yet for a time at least it looked as if the avant-garde wing of the National Socialist movement might win. Benn's *Confession of Faith in Expressionism* captures this moment in time and is also an interesting attempt by him to prove that Expressionism and National Socialism are not incompatible. The essay can unfortunately be given here only in a shortened form, which does not quite show the full extent of Benn's accommodation to Nazi racialist thinking. But enough still remains to give the flavour of the time.

Benn starts by attempting to prove that the modern art movement was racially pure. He singles out Fascists like Hanns Johst and Marinetti for special mention and even enlists Goethe, Kleist and Nietzsche as respectable forerunners of the movement. Wagner too is mentioned, but not for his Germanic fantasies. Instead Benn interprets him as an exponent of 'absolute' music and reminds the reader of his 'flights into stages of primal being'. He admits that the Expressionists were obsessed with the destruction of reality and much given to visions and ecstatic, trance-like states, but for this too he finds respectable ancestors in German mystics like Meister Eckhart and Jakob Böhme and even improbably links the names of Schiller, Bach and Dürer together to prove his point. It goes without saying that the humanitarian, social and pacifistic aspects of Expressionism (by any other reckoning its strongest side) are totally denied and anti-liberal tendencies claimed for it. His final plea is against the common charges that Expressionism was intellectual and destructive, unintelligible and subjective, formalistic and apolitical. This proves extremely difficult for the charges were largely true and Benn himself was guilty of most of them. However, although there is no denying how slanted his view of Expressionism was, there is equally no denying his allegiance to it. This was indeed the artistic generation to which he belonged no matter how ambivalent his attitude to it.

His *Novel of the Phenotype* has little in common with the traditional expectation of plot, character, and so on associated with that label. Instead his is an

49

exercise in 'absolute prose', outside of time and space and devoid of individual psychology and development. Absolute prose was a literary possibility he had discussed in various essays already, modelling himself on Pascal, Flaubert and Gide (*Paludes*). But this was also a problem much discussed by the Expressionists and Benn himself quotes Carl Einstein's novel *Bebuquin* (1912) which was then a widely discussed exercise in this type of prose in the 1920's. Like so many Expressionists Benn had nothing but contempt for the traditional novel and confidently predicted its demise. Of course, it has not died and it is Benn's own absolute prose that has so far failed to establish itself as a viable form. Benn's other exercise in this vein, *The Ptolomean* (1947), is a magnificent exercise in experimental prose from many points of view. But it too did not fundamentally influence the direction of the German narrative. However, it did provide the German public with a wonderful split-level model of how to survive successfully in a world without beliefs. The model is the Ptolomean himself who, as a beautician, lives in the world of appearances with one half of his being and in the 'real' world of the mind with the other. This double life is summed up in the work itself in slogans of typical Benn-type brilliance. Of these the one which became most current in Germany was 'Erkenne die Lage'—realise the true position. In *Double Life* Benn went into greater detail of what he meant by this: if you can realise the position, you can adjust accordingly, accommodate, assume a protective colouring, avoid convictions which pin you down too much. On the other hand, if institutions and organisations demand convictions, ideologies, and so on, you go along with them as far as is necessary. As usual

Benn is being disturbingly ambivalent. He quickly makes it clear that he is not talking about moral decisions, he is personally only concerned with the position of the artist who must keep his head free for the creation of *forms*. But as usual in ethical as distinct from aesthetic terms his kind of divided existence offered a distinctly dangerous solution to the alienating pressures of modern life. The dilemma he points to does, however, show fascinating similarities to that of Bert Brecht who was also constantly forced to construct split personalities like Shen Te/Shui Ta and Azdak the good/bad judge in order to show the impossibility of resolving the extreme poles of modern life.

The tone of these works is now that of an old man and the wisdom of the East plays an ever increasing rôle. In his later years Benn became almost obsessed with the question of old age—and of survival. Not that there could be any question of any last minute conversion. He was merely amused by the avant-garde writers who, like Döblin, suddenly found faith. Once again Flaubert was his model : 'Je suis mystique et je ne crois à rien'.

Turning from the prose to the poetry means going back to the period before the First World War when Benn first burst upon the literary scene. The author himself has given his account of how he first gained the reputation of being a terrible coffee-house littérateur whereas he was in fact very much still the military officer. But the reception of the poems themselves is far more interesting than how Benn came to write them. They had been passed to A. R. Meyer in manuscript form together with a pile of others being considered for publication. But these were so confused that Meyer was tempted to throw the whole lot aside after a cursory glance. Then right at the end he came across this cycle of poems which were so different from all the others he had to shout out loud in excitement. These poems were based on real (medical) experience and not just on literature. The cycle was called *Morgue* and the individual poems were 'Little Aster', 'Happy Youth', 'Circulation', 'Nigger Bride', 'Requiem', 'Labour Ward', 'Appendix', 'Man and Woman go through a Cancer Ward' and 'All Night Café'. The pamphlet with these poems was set up and printed in eight days; it bears the date March 1912. It is doubtful if the press in Germany has ever reacted to poetry in such an expressive, explosive manner as it did to these few poems. One famous critic gave Benn the name 'Hellhound Breughel' in honour of this recital of horrors. A newspaper review thundered:

Disgraceful! What an unbridled imagination devoid of all mental hygiene is here laid bare; what disgusting delight in the abysmally ugly, what nasty pleasure in dragging into the light of day things which cannot be altered.

Another reviewer wrote:

If you intend to read these ... poems, get a stiff drink ready beforehand, a very, very stiff drink! ! !

Only the *Berlin Post* seems to have realised that a new star had arisen (but then Berlin was different from the rest of Germany!). It wrote:

At last a poet has been found to lift our future out of triviality and point us in the direction of high goals. Goethe must now abandon his place on Mount Olympus: another will take his place and that man is Gottfried Benn. We may think ourselves lucky to be born into an age in which such a poet lives.

Such praise and abuse may seem excessive on the basis of a few poems, but extreme reactions to Benn's poetry were to be the norm throughout his career in Germany.

Probably the poems of the *Morgue* cycle no longer have the power to shock. The modern reader is long since immune to such horrors. But the casual tone in which Benn dispenses beauty and ugliness with equal objectivity and irony does still have considerable impact. The poems are always disturbing, and Benn makes sure that no one will simply like them. They are not *nice*. 'Little Aster' is a typical example. The corpse with a flower between its teeth is deliberately grotesque and surrealistic, but for the chest cavity to be used as a vase even more so. And still more gruesome is the image of the flower sliding into the brain! There is irony too in the last words—'Rest in peace'—addressed, not to the drowned driver, but to the flower in its new vase. Hence what could have been rather a naturalistic recital of horrors has in fact become an expressionistic poem reaching out into extremely disturbing realms.

The poem 'Happy Youth' also exploits material much used by the Expressionist generation, namely the Ophelia theme. Heym had written a very similar poem, and Brecht too was later to develop the theme in 'The Ballad of the Drowned Girl'. In Benn's poem the contrast of beauty and ugliness is consciously stressed and as in the previous poem, 'Little Aster', there is an ironic twist to the last few words, for they make the title 'Happy Youth' apply not to the poor deserted maiden whose life has ended in the water, but to the rats who have been joyfully living off her body!

But perhaps the most horrific of the poems in the

little *Morgue* cycle is the one called 'Man and Woman go through a Cancer Ward'. Despite the ghastliness of the horrors exposed in the poem the tone is the cool, conversational one of the doctor who daily confronts this spectacle of mass death and decay. He seems emotionally uninvolved, having witnessed it all a hundred times, though this may be only a professional mask over his real feelings. As he leads the woman through the ward, demonstrating the various types of decaying flesh, so the reader too is *forced* to look at everything closely: that lump of fat and foul juices that once was a woman, for example. He is made to feel, while the patients remain unaware. They are all drugged, unconscious. For all their sores they feel nothing, they do not suffer. But if the patients feel nothing while the reader does, what is the nature of the feelings evoked in the reader? What does Benn intend by insisting on horrors which undeniably exist, even though in the past they had never been considered suitable material for poetic treatment? Is his attitude really one of complete indifference? Does he merely wish to disgust and shock, *pour épater le bourgeois*? Or does he follow the Naturalist example of showing such suffering in order to enlist the sympathy of the audience with the despairing suggestion that something ought to be done? Or does Benn select terminal cases because so often nothing can be done, because there is no solution to the problem of inevitable death and decay? Benn's poem remains typically ambivalent. He pretends to be hard and indifferent, but one senses that he is deeply moved. What he shows is not the, perhaps, meaningful suffering of the individual, but the general process. He seems to be demonstrating the insignificance of private feelings.

Take love, for example. He indicates what that comes to by pointing to the woman whose body, now a mass of fat and foul humours, had once meant home and ecstasy for some man. Even at this very early stage the later Benn is significantly foreshadowed, for already he sees things in terms of the cosmic vision, as the last lines of the poem shows :

> Here the land is swirling up around each bed.
> Flesh subsides to soil. Red heat dies off.
> Sap starts to trickle. The earth is calling.

Even the big city ambience of the 'All Night Café' with its pimpled youths and prostitutes can give rise to an equally mystic experience. The key-word in this poem as in 'Little Aster' is 'brain', for it is this that feels the presence of woman :

> Woman. Desert dried out. Canaanite brown.
> Chaste. Full of caves. A scent comes with her.
> Hardly scent. It's only a sweet leaning forward
>   of the air against my brain.

This is no naturalistic or impressionistic recording of reality. This is an attempt to express a vision in words.

It is this same vision of woman as a possible means of escape from the isolation and brain weariness of the individual that is conjured up in 'Express Train' (1912), a title that has echoes of Stadler's famous expressionistic poem 'On Crossing the Rhine at Cologne by Night'. But what Benn's poem offers is the almost primitive fury of the sexual encounter ('Male brown hurls itself upon female brown') such as one finds in Kokoschka's *Murderer Hope of Womankind*. It is significant too how often Benn draws attention to the curse of thought (brain, brow, neck, etc.) contrasted with the blood, both in this poem and the next, 'Subway Train' (1913). In the latter the connections with the subway are by no means clear, but there is no doubting the power of the natural and sexual imagery. Yet even stronger is the longing for freedom from the affliction of thought through regression. Instead of being a wretched brain dog laden down with God, he would become vegetable matter, instead of thinking—he would 'swell and stream and shudder'. So the awesome regression would continue all the way back to 'shadows and flood. For joys: a languid dying down into ocean's deep redeeming blue.'

The most cogent expression to this longing for regression is given in Benn's 'Songs I and II' (1913). The affliction of thought is so great that to escape from it he would rather go back through the aeons of time to the very beginnings of life on this planet. Life then meant an organism in a swamp—anything more advanced than that would already be on the path to awareness—and to suffering. The second part continues the cosmic framework against which human emotions like hope and despair seem contemptible indeed. This does not, however, necessarily imply an attitude of pessimism. Benn did discuss pessimism at various points in his career. Generally speaking he came out ambivalently neither for nor against. As with the question of nihilism, the main point is that pessimism should be fruitful. Hebbel too could be said to have had a pessimistic view of the world, but his basic response was always to create, no matter how badly things turned against him. In his portrait poem 'Young Hebbel' (1913) Benn might almost have been describing his own poetry, for he too reacted against the fine nuances (in his case of a Rilke or a Hofmannsthal) and preferred instead to chisel out FORM with his own head. The word *Stirn* (forehead) for Benn generally implies brain; and the word 'form' is also highly important here for this was to be his answer to the potential chaos he saw around him. His is not only intellectual, but also extremely formalistic poetry. The second stanza brings a further concept which is fundamental for an understanding of Benn's poetry. The focus not only on the blood yet again, but also on the 'I'. The ego wants to realise its full potential and uncover the self buried in the *blood,* capable of creating worlds of its own. Why is he so ugly? Because his young life is like a scab with a wound underneath oozing blood every day. But the response yet again is not pessimism but unremitting struggle to create form out of chaos, beauty out of ugliness.

As Hamburger has pointed out, there is little linguistic difficulty or extravagance about Benn's early poetry. The cool detached tone, the occasional medical jargon and the deliberately colloquial insolence presented no difficulties for the reader even though the poems often opened up into cosmic and visionary reaches. Benn did not employ any of the more extreme linguistic experiments of his Expressionist contemporaries. In poems like 'Icarus' (1915) and 'Caryatid' (1916), however, this is no longer the case. The range of subject matter is as wide as ever, if not wider, especially in its extension to classical mythology, and the imagery is far from immediately obvious. Commenting on this poem in which they see Benn emerging as the Expressionist poet of the subliminal, Hamburger and Middleton remark first upon the obscurity of the image of the essential Silenus at large in the living soul and then go on :

'Caryatid' also has other important implications: the poem suggests that only the human imagination can emancipate man from the stony fixity of his actual state; but finally even

57

this belief is put in doubt, for the moment of ecstasy is a *Glück-Lügenstunde* ('moment of joy and lie'). In this typical *parole essentielle,* the ecstasy and the doubt merge and are fixed. Nonetheless, the idea of transcendent imagination underlies the whole of Benn's subsequent work, its irrationalism strangely consorting with a phrasing so urbane and a diction so near-scientific.

This combination of irrationalism, urbane phrasing and scientific jargon was to be the Benn trade-mark from now on. Sometimes, however, the 'counterfeit bliss how' will not come, sometimes there is no natural escape from the devouring brain and the dreamlike state or trance must be sought through drugs as in 'Cocain' (1917):

> Sweet deep desired disintegration of what was me,
> Is yours to give: my throat feels rough sensations,
> Deep down strange echoes are at work already
> On my mind's unspoken creations.

'O Night' (1916), another poem of the same time, also strives to attain the primal vision (das Ur), the paradisal state, the concentrated essence of being which the brain and the dream by themselves are incapable of attaining:

> Oh night, I was already on cocain
> The blood rush is already under way
> My hair turns grey, the years begin to wane
> I must, I must in ecstasy
> Bloom once more before passing away.

The unusual five-line stanza is not continued in the rest of the poem which follows Benn's favourite pattern of the four-line stanza with alternating rhymes and regular rhythm.

The poem 'The Singer' (1925) reads like a statement of his concept of the poet and indeed being so 'self'-centred Benn does in fact often write about the problems of poetic creation. The striking feature of this poem is the vocabulary Benn is prepared to use, not simply *paroles essentielles* like *Glücklügenstunde* or *Südlichkeit* as in 'Caryatid', but very scientific, technical words like hyperaemia and azimuth. Such 'unpoetic' language has a certain shock effect, but once its meaning has been grasped and its potential for poetry admitted, it can be seen that Benn is once again widening the range of his lyrical expressivity. The basic technique of the poem seems akin to the Expressionistic one of *montage*, whereby a series of substantives are placed in explosive proximity to each other. (There are very few adjectives : a poem of this kind is not striving for shades of meaning or fine nuances.) Similarly there are very few finite verbs. Any suggestion of action, movement or direction is carefully avoided. Already such poems tend towards the 'static', one of the key concepts for Benn's later poetry. When the various substantives in the poem are examined, they are seen to have been all carefully chosen to spark off their own world of associations. Hence although in the expressionistic manner the poem is very condensed and concentrated it is also capable of vast scope.

Benn's singer or poet brings vastly different spheres together : germs, the very beginnings of intellectual concepts, Broadways (the plural indicates not the real place, but the type of place in the jazzy twentieth-century world), astronomical relationships, the obscurities of our primeval past; and all this he masters by means of the word, not as a rational process, but by mysteriously compounding them in his blood. As an exponent of word magic his endeavour is to give them form, expression, and what this absolute form aims at is that state of momentary escape that drugs, dreams,

59

trances, 'southernness' perhaps could also give—the counterfeit bliss of forgetfulness of the real state of affairs. In reality the universe is characterised by a total lack of harmony, the isolation of the individual is absolute, there is no bridge over the gap between I and you. If the first stanza reveals the duality of the world with intellect, reason, scientific and mathematical concepts on the one hand and the primitive world and the blood on the other, it is clear from the second stanza that Benn now accepts this situation. Progressive cerebration is the path of the modern poet. By this means he can liberate the archetypal visions which are imprisoned in the cervical cortex. Hence the modern poem is neurogenous, i.e. a product of nervous and intellectual tensions. Hyperaemia, on the other hand, is the opposite of anaemia. The poem is therefore the product of a rush of blood to the brain induced by drugs. Where once the poet had been a dualist, i.e. aware of the lack of harmony in the universe, but creating his own personal synthesis (like Rilke and Hofmannsthal), now he is a destroyer by means of the intellect. Operating always on the cosmic scale, pressing his difficult materials into the dream of the poem. All this he pushes along slowly and only rarely does he succeed in creating a true poem, but when he does what it demonstrates is pure artistry. Absolute art. It expresses the void, the total nihilism of which the modern poet is aware.

'The Singer' is not a great lyrical masterpiece in its own right, but it does warn the reader of the kind of poetry to expect from Benn. It warns him not only of the 'difficult substances' he will use in his poetry, it gives some indication of how Benn approaches the task of writing poetry. Modern poems, then, according to Benn are made, they are distilled essences, they reveal the chaotic surge of existence ('Ecstatic Stream', 1927), but through statuesque form. They are themselves static (*Statische Gedichte*). But always he goes back to the primitive, exotic world of magic and incantation where 'all that still holds and stays also longs for destruction down to the limbless stage, down to the vacuum, back to the primal age, dark ocean's womb'. Such oceanic poetry seems nearer to Georg Kaiser's drama *The Coral*, with its hectic flight from the self, than to Brecht's exotic tales. But there are in fact constant reminders of Brecht throughout Benn's poetry. They both shared the same love for sporting terms like 'finish' and 'come-back', they both love the exotic-erotic associations of the harbour and far away places with strange sounding names from Alaska to Palau, Benn had even at one time written a cycle of poems about Alaska, but it is the Mediterranean and southern poems which have had the greater impact, while the North American echoes are largely overlooked. Benn himself wrote on the subject of Americanism in *Transition* (1928) in the following terms:

I shall limit myself to discussing literature. In this, its influence, as far as post-war Germany is concerned, is enormous. There is a group of lyric poets, who think they have composed a poem, by writing 'Manhattan'. There is a group of playwrights, who think they reveal the modern drama by having the action take place in an Arizona blockhouse and by having a bottle of whisky on the table. The entire German literature since 1918 is working under the slogan of tempo, jazz, cinema, overseas, technical activity by emphasizing the negation of an ensemble of psychic problems. The influence of Americanism is so enormous, because it is analogous in certain tendencies with other currents forming the young current of today: Marxism, the materialistic philosophy of history, the purely animalistic social doctrine, Communism, whose common attacks are directed against the individualistic and the metaphysical being.

Personally I am against Americanism. I am of the opinion that the philosophy of purely utilitarian thinking, of optimism à tout prix, of 'keep smiling', of the perpetual grin upon the teeth, does not suit the Occidental man and his history. I hope that the European, at least in the pure types of his artists, will always reject the purely utilitarian, the mass article, the collective plan, and that he will live only from within himself.

Despite the occasionally quaint English this statement is not only typical of Benn, it almost sounds as if it were directed against Brecht who was both a Marxist and a lover of exotic Americana. Yet in a poem written about the same time 'Qui Sait' (1927) and dedicated to Carl Sternheim who was as obsessed as Brecht with Capitalist go-getters and the American scene, Benn shows the extent to which consciously or unconsciously the phenomenon of America had coloured his own language and imagery. The Hoboken quay, Pacific power plant, even Henry Clay cigars make the poem sound like an echo of Brecht's own vision of the destruction of the cities in 'Of Poor B.B.'.

(Thus we built those tall boxes on the island of Manhattan
And those thin antennae that amuse the Atlantic swell.)
Of those cities will remain: what passed through them, the wind!

The transience of things is, of course, an ancient theme of lyrical poetry. With Benn it is taken to its ultimate conclusion when he accuses life itself of being empty, as the title of the poem 'Life—a base Illusion' (1927) indicates. Who is the 'you' being addressed in this poem? Poet, German, twentieth-century white man? Life in any event is not for him. Life, Benn suggests elsewhere, is really lived by the primitive races, not by the modern intellectual. Here life is dismissed as a base illusion, a dream for children and serfs, and not presumably for the heroic individual. The ancient stock being addressed is a representative of a race that has come to the end of its course—a widely held belief in the twenties and thirties when the Russians and the Asiatic races (like the working classes) were thought to have somehow preserved all the vitality that the decadent, careful, thinking middle-classes lacked. But Benn uses not only such Spenglerian language of racial and cultural doom, he is still a pastor's son and this poem like some others has many Christian echoes. He first rejects momentary solutions to the problem of life such as he had found before, namely *Berauschung,* i.e. intoxication in which the barriers separating the individual from the world are broken down. Likewise he rejects the solution through love, whereby the I and the you, i.e. man and woman, come together as one. He also rejects religious solutions through faith and deeds. In the end one possibility alone remains as an absolute constant in an otherwise illusory world—form.

The secret of form is the theme of 'He who is alone' (1936). He who is alone (and thus free of all associations, beliefs, contacts) is initiated into the secret, he can break through the surface and see the world as it really is, he is intellectually and physically aware, 'pregnant' with the vision of chaos. The world is in flux and human life (which Benn reduces to two basic functions, eating and mating) is doomed to destruction. Without feeling, he watches the world—this is the familiar detached attitude of the doctor or the dandy, the characteristic attitude of the modern poet like Sternheim, who never indulges in emotional outbursts. Without feeling he watches the world change into something different from what he had known. But that does not mean development, improvement, progress; and this is the significance of the distorted Goethe quotation: Goethe's famous words 'Stirb und Werde' become 'Nicht mehr stirb und werde'—there is no rebirth! The distorted quotation is a technical device used with equal virtuosity by Erich Kästner, T. S. Eliot or Bert Brecht. But whatever the context, the effect is always the same, namely to highlight the conflict between former high ideals and modern reality. The poem ends on a quiet note with the characteristic Expressionist tension between form and chaos: 'Formstill sieht ihn die Vollendung an.' (He meets the gaze of perfection's tranquil form.)

Benn rather enjoys the pose of himself as the lonely poet, even identifying his own personal loneliness with the existential state of modern man. At the same time his pose is sometimes not far removed from the National Socialist Ideal of the Hitlerian hero fighting his lonely battles, as in the poem of the thirties, 'Seeing the Swords never Falter':

> The common sociological factor
> Through the centuries asleep
> Reads: one or two great leaders
> Whose suffering was deep.

This makes the whole theme banal and sentimental, and banality and sentimentality were dangers which Benn did not always escape. It must be said of Benn that even at the height of his intoxication with National Socialism he never indulged in poetic eulogies of the Führer or the party. He was simply not that kind of poet.

In his lecture 'Problems of Lyrical Poetry' he was

later to discourse at length on the ideal poem as he saw it and this was definitely not poetry for any faith or political party. He spoke of 'the absolute poem, the poem without faith, the poem without hope, the poem addressed to no one, the poem made of words assembled in a fascinating way'. It may be seriously questioned whether Benn or any other modern poet has ever realised this ideal, but one or two examples of sheer magic like 'Wave of the Night' (1943) and 'One Word' (1943) force the reader to stop looking for the meaning (though the poems are of course not devoid of meaning) and experience the rhythm, the rhyme, the formal excellence and the lucidity of the images, whether Mediterranean or cosmic, captured by the power of the poetic word.

Always Benn returns to the theme of the self, so the most often anthologised and also the most untranslatable of his poems is 'Verlorenes Ich' 'The Lost "I" ', 1943). The last stanzas of this difficult poem give by *montage* a vision of the lost age of harmony when man lived in a world which had one centre in God, in faith. But this final vision of a happier time only serves to reinforce the dreadful situation of modern man who has been shaken and uprooted by the knowledge of infinity provided by modern science. Infinity had been an abstract concept which troubled but few thinkers. Modern science has made it into an entity which enters into everybody's lives. Hence man has no firm centre any longer, he is exploded by the infinite vastness of the cosmos and the infinite minuteness of the ion, the smallest particle of matter. He is the sacrificial lamb of death rays : the terms particle and field, are taken from modern physics to demonstrate the infinite forces to which he is exposed and over which he has no control.

The last line of the first stanza with its reference to Notre Dame, another sphere in which infinities are embodied, is a typical juxtaposition of apparent opposites, science and religion.

In the second stanza the possibility of escape from this isolating awareness is posited, namely escape from oneself into normal activity. The 'world' can be a flight. Empty time conceals the infinite. But even here the questions still demand an answer: Where do you end up? Where are you? Where are your points of contact? Loss or gain? Have these words any meaning? It is all a game played by beasts—you flee along the walls of these eternities—you cannot escape from them.

The next stanza presents considerable linguistic difficulties. What is implied by 'gaze of the beast: the stars are butchers' lights'? Despite such obscurities the general meaning is clear—man, great battles, events in history like the encounter on the fields of Châlons (A.D. 451) of which it has always been said that it saved Europe from the Asiatic hordes: all these things are meaningless when weighed against the infinities of which modern man is aware. Man, history, places and times, heroes and great deeds of the past, all are meaningless, empty, all plunge down the bestial gullet.

The next stanza gives the source of the present mental state in the typical Benn formula, 'Die Welt zerdacht'. The prefix 'zer' indicates destructive force, hence it means the world has been destroyed, thought has removed all possibility of harmony in the universe. Space and time and all things which once moved mankind are now the 'functions' of infinities. In the past man's thought had been directed to God, it had a centre, now thought is independent, it explains the universe in terms of abstractions which in turn man can no longer grasp. They are beyond his scope. Whereas formerly the myth had given a picture of the universe which primitive man could appreciate—he knew where he was in the scheme of things—now he is told that the myth was false and man is left only with the awareness of his cosmic isolation. Modern man is utterly lost.

This is one of Benn's most famous poems, though not perhaps one of his most successful. What makes it most striking and effective (and also virtually untranslatable —at least into the same metre and rhymes) is the extreme use of the expressionistic techniques in it, particularly *montage* which forces the awareness of the fragmentation of the world upon the reader. Not only does the poem bristle with scientific jargon, it is characterised by extreme condensation and compression. Here as in the earlier poems, the finite verb is practically eliminated, and substantives are strung together. Associative links are virtually non-existent and the reader is left to cope with encyclopaedic references of cosmic dimensions.

But by no means all of Benn's poetry is so Alexandrian and learned. In fact as he grew older Benn turned more and more to simple direct language to express his ideas and attitudes, as for example in the collection *Static Poems* (1948) which starts as follows:

> Avoidance of evolution
> Is the wise man's deepest insight,
> Children and children's children
> Do not disturb him,
> Do not impinge upon him.
>
> To advocate courses of action,
> Do something,
> Journey hither and thither
> Is the mark of a world
> Which does not see clearly.

Outside my window
—the wise man says—
Lies a valley,
In which the shadows gather,
Two poplars mark the edge of a path
Going—you know where.

This particular poem does continue in much more technical language, but the return to colloquial style is clearly noticeable. The fragmentation of modern existence which had been the theme of 'Lost I' is expressed in much simpler terms in the poem 'Fragments' (1950) and the journeying theme of the poem just quoted becomes the theme of the poem 'Travel, (1950) which could not be simpler in language. The later Benn is characterised by this gradual abandoning of Expressionistic extremes and a return to almost traditional elegiac forms and tones. Benn takes the traditional theme of the lonely wanderer and expresses it in his characteristically ironic terms. For him the modern traveller is a tourist and the poem sounds at the start like an absolutely realistic discussion in a Travel Agency. The rhythm is at first that of normal speech in which everything beyond the world of concrete reality (miracles and consecrations) is questioned. Does anybody really believe that one place (say Zurich) can be 'deeper' than another, does anybody really believe that a place can offer something to fill up one's life, to give it real substance (Inhalt). Europe is full of holy places, South America is more exotic. But the modern world remains a wasteland, modern man's life remains hollow. Rushing round famous cities will not give anyone's life a significance it did not have before. After the conversational tone of the questions in the first two stanzas the recital of famous place names forces home the message of the emptiness of modern life and the burden of the last lines is the return to the resigned wisdom of the 'Static Poem', namely to stay put and preserve the self-sufficient ego, knowing that the only reality is death. Modern man like Kafka's Starvation Artist hungers for a food that does not exist!

There is no escaping now the note of tired acceptance which the poems of the older Benn exude, a note decidedly more pleasing than his pose of heroic isolation in the face of the void. He no longer sees himself as the nihilistic superman of superhuman suffering. Now as in 'Notturno' (1951) he sits in the pub quietly smoking and drinking and his soul finds peace. After all, 'no man's suffering ever went beyond six feet deep. And that's not much.' The pub is where we find him too in the poem 'Restaurant' (1950) engaged in a dialogue about death. But thinking and talking about death do not make anybody unique. As he says in 'Sentence Structure' (1951), everybody has heaven, love and death, the culture vultures have well and truly worked them over. The really pressing question is why do we try to express anything?

> What is the meaning of these urges,
> Part image, part word and calculation,
> What is in you, whence these surges,
> Of still and sorrowful sensation?
>
> ('Poem' 1955)

This is the question Benn's work poses. This compulsion to write poems is what gives his life substance. Did it make him a great poet? Probably not. A great thinker? Certainly not. He was a man who followed many spiritual leaders: Hebbel, Nietzsche, Flaubert, Heinrich Mann, and others. Perhaps he came nearest to Chopin, the musician whom he admired most, who:

69

Never composed an opera,
Not one symphony,
only these tragic progressions
from artistic conviction
and with a tiny hand.

TRANSLATIONS

PROSE

ITHACA

Characters:
ALBRECHT, *a professor of pathology*
DR. RÖNNE, *his assistant*
Medical Students
KAUTSKI, *a student*
LUTZ, *a student*

In the professor's laboratory. At the end of a course. The professor and medical students.

PROFESSOR: And now, gentlemen, to the special surprise I have saved for you as a final treat. As you see here, having stained pyramidal cells from the cornu ammonis in the left hemisphere of the cervical cortex of a fourteen day rat of a special strain, what do we find—they are stained not red but pink with a tinge of brownish violet, just verging on green. A most fascinating observation. You are aware that not long ago the Graz Institute brought out a paper disputing this, notwithstanding the detailed nature of my own investigations on this subject. Far be it from me to make any general comment on the Graz Institute, but I must say that the paper in question struck me as immature in the extreme. And now, as you see, I have the proof here in front of me. The possibilities this opens up are quite staggering. One would be able to tell rats with long black hair and dark eyes from those with short rough hair and light eyes by the additional means of this sensitive colour-index, given that the rats are similar in age, fed on candy-sugar, that they play for half an hour daily with a puma kitten and defecate spontaneously twice nightly at a body temperature of 37.36°C. Naturally, the fact that similar phenomena have also been observed under other conditions

73

must not be ignored, but even so this observation seems to me worth publishing in full—indeed, I would almost regard it as a new step towards the understanding of the vast complex of forces which control the universe. And so, good evening, gentlemen, good evening.

LUTZ: And supposing, Professor, that one does examine this preparation carefully, can one say anything more than: I see, so this is not red, but pink, tinged with brownish violet, verging on green?

PROFESSOR: Gentlemen, please! In the first place there is the three volume encyclopedia by Meyer and Müller on the staining of rats' brains. As a first step one would have to go through that.

LUTZ: And supposing that was done, would it be possible to draw any conclusions? To come up with practical consequences?

PROFESSOR: Conclusions! My good man, we are not Thomas Aquinas, ha ha ha! Have you never heard of the new age of conditionalism which has dawned for our science? We establish the conditions in which something happens. We vary the conditions which make certain changes possible Theology is a different case entirely.

LUTZ: And supposing one day your whole student audience got to its feet and bellowed at you that it would prefer mysticism of the blackest hue to the dusty creakings of your mental acrobatics, suppose they sent you flying from the rostrum with a kick in the backside, what would you say to that? (*Enter Dr. Rönne.*)

RÖNNE: Here is your book on the perforation of the peritoneum in infants. I have no interest whatsoever in describing the state of an abdominal cavity as found on autopsy to an audience of people I do not know, already trained in what to expect. And my brain revolts at this game, this wish to destroy, to break up the simple, self-contained naïvety of an individual case.

PROFESSOR: Your reasons are foolish in the extreme, but as you wish, give it to me. There are plenty other gentlemen interested in the paper. If you were rather less short-sighted than you seem to be in my opinion, you would understand that it's not a question of this individual case. On the contrary with every particular examination the systematisation of all knowledge, the organisation of experience—in a word, science itself is at stake.

RÖNNE: Science had its rightful place two hundred years ago when it could prove God's wisdom from the perfection of organs and the extent of His intelligence and goodness from the mouths of locusts. But in two hundred years from now, Professor, will it not seem just as ludicrous that you spend three years of your life establishing whether the stain to be used on a particular type of fat is osmium or Nile blue.

PROFESSOR: I have not the slightest intention of discussing general principles with you. You do not wish to do this piece of work. Right, I shall give you another one.

RÖNNE: Nor do I wish to describe the result of the catheter-isation of Frau Schmidt's uterus—whether the intestinal coils passed through the gap in question in the sixth or the eighth month. Nor to tell them how much the diaphragm of a drowned man was distended next morning. The collection, the systematisation of knowledge—is the most puerile brainwork imaginable! For a century now you have been encouraging the stupidity of the population to the point where the plebs will gawp in respectful silence at any old B.F. who knows how to work an incubation chamber, but in so doing you have yet to come up with as much as a grain of thought of less than total banality. Get one lot hatched after another; keep your thoughts on the navel and don't forget the placenta—that's all you can think of—you bunch of moles and ape-brains—you make me spew, the lot of you!

LUTZ: What are you really doing? Now and again you grab up a fact, so-called. In the first place it's been discovered already, but not published, by a colleague ten years ago. Another ten years and it'll all be in the dustbin. And what do you really know? That earthworms don't need knives and forks and ferns don't get sores on their backsides. That's the extent of your achievements. Is there anything else you know?

PROFESSOR: In the first place, it is completely beneath my dignity to reply to the tone of your remarks.

LUTZ: Dignity? Whose dignity? Who are you? Go on, answer.

PROFESSOR: I'll frame my reply to suit the occasion. Right, gentlemen, you talk disparagingly about theories, that's no concern of mine. But in a subject of such eminently practical implications: you must admit that serum and salvarsan are not just speculation?

LUTZ: Are you trying to argue that what you're working for is to let Frau Meier do her daily shopping for two months longer or to let Krause, the chauffeur, carry on at the wheel for another two months? Anyway, if that is what you enjoy, the fight to keep these nobodies alive, you carry on. And just to forestall you, Professor, don't bring up the argument about the universal human drive. There are whole civilisations where the people lie in the sand all day playing bamboo flutes.

PROFESSOR: And humane values? Saving a child's life for its mother or a breadwinner's for his family? The gratitude shining in their eyes.

RÖNNE: Let it shine, Professor! Infant mortality and every other kind are as much a part of life as winter is of the year. Don't let us reduce Life to trivialities.

LUTZ: Anyway these practical aspects are of very superficial interest. The question which we want to hear answered is this: Where do you get the courage to introduce youth to a science which you know to be incapable of any greater insight than a confession of its own ignorance? Just because it suits your shit-like lump of a brain to work out the statistics of bowel-blockages when you're not hard at it fucking? What kind of brains do you think you've got in front of you?

PROFESSOR: . . .

RÖNNE: . . . O.K! O.K! The commanding heights of the intellect! A thousand years of optics and chemistry! O.K! O.K! there are not so many colour-blind people in the world, so you have a certain advantage. But let me tell you, I've stomached your lies till they make me sick—if you dare to come out with them just once more I shall strangle you with my own hands. I've chewed the whole cosmos to pieces inside my head. I've sat and thought till I slavered at the mouth. I've been so out and out logical I nearly vomited shit. And once the mists had cleared, what was left? Words and the brain. Over and over again this same terrifying, everlasting brain. Nailed to this cross. Caught in this incest. In this rape of things—if you only knew my existence, this torment, this terrible sense that we're at an end, betrayed before God by the beasts, and God and beast alike destroyed by thought and spewed out, a random throw in the mists of this land, I tell you you would resign quietly without fuss and be glad that you are not being called to account for the brain damage you have caused.

PROFESSOR: I am extremely sorry if you should be feeling unwell. But if your degeneracy or neurosis or for all I know these medieval mists of yours are causing you to go to pieces, what has that got to do with me? Why get worked up at me? If you really haven't got the strength to join us on the road to the new knowledge, why not just stay behind? Give up your anatomy. Go in for mysticism. Use formulae and corollaries to calculate the location of the soul; but leave us out of it. We are spread out over the world like an army: heads to rule with and brains to conquer with. The force that cut axes from stone, that kept fire alive, that gave birth to Kant, that created machines—is ours to conserve. The prospects ahead are infinite.

RÖNNE: The prospects ahead infinite; an enormous cervical cortex with a fold in the middle takes a little stroll; fingers stand up like calipers; teeth have grown into computers—mankind will turn into a maw with a machine on top, systematising—what perspectives! What infinite perspectives ahead! For all I care we could have stayed jelly-fish. For me the whole history of evolution is useless. The brain is a blind alley. A bluff to fool the middle-classes. Whether one walks vertically or swims horizontally is all a matter of habit. The totality of life, its overall structures have been destroyed for me by thought. The cosmos roars past on its way. I stand on the bank: grey, steep, barren. My branches hang down into the living water; but their gaze is turned inwards, on the waning flow of their blood and the numbing chill in their limbs. I am set apart, my self. I make no move now.

Where, where will it lead? Why make the long journey? What centre is there for us to gather round? When I stopped thinking for a moment, surely my limbs fell off?

Something finds associations inside one. Some process takes place inside one. All I can feel now is my brain. It lies on my skull like a lichen. It gives me from above a feeling of nausea. It lies everywhere ready to pounce: yellow, yellow, brain, brain. It hangs down between my legs ... I can feel it distinctly knocking against my ankles.

Oh, if I could return to the state of being of a grassy field,

sand dotted with flowers, a vast meadow. With the earth
bearing everything to one on waves that are warm or cool.
No forehead left. A state of being lived.

KAUTSKI: But can you not see the dawn all around our
bodies? There since eternity, since the primal stage of the
world? A century is at an end. A sickness is conquered. A
dark journey, the sails straining; now the music of home is
heard across the sea.

Who is to say what has driven you away? A curse, the
Fall, or something else. For thousands of years there were no
more than mere beginnings of it. For thousands of years it lay
hidden. But then, a century ago it suddenly exploded and like
a pestilence engulfed the world till nothing was left but that
animal, large, greedy and power-hungry: the man of intellect;
he stretched from heaven to heaven, he conjured the world
out of his mind. But we are older. We are blood; from the
warm seas, the mothers who gave birth to life. You are a
small channel of this same sea. Come home now. I call you.

PROFESSOR: Don't let Rönne mislead you. All this thinking
with no clearly defined objective has crushed him. Such
casualties will be inevitable on our path.

RÖNNE: The Mediterranean was there; from primeval times;
and it is there still. Perhaps it is the most human thing there
has ever been? What do you think? . . .

PROFESSOR: (Continuing) But, gentlemen, all these strange
feelings and the other things you talked about—myth and
knowledge, could it not be that these are age-old poisons in
our bloodstream, which will be cast off in the course of
evolution, just as we no longer possess a third eye looking
backwards to warn us of enemies. In the hundred years
during which the sciences and their application have existed,
how life has changed! Has not Man's mental activity largely
abandoned speculation and the transcendental to concentrate
entirely on the shaping of material things, to satisfy the needs
of a self-renewing soul? Is it not already possible to talk
about a homo faber instead of a homo sapiens as hitherto? Is
it not right that in the course of time all Man's speculative-
transcendental needs will be refined and purified out of
existence? Could scientific research and the teaching of knowledge not be justified from that point of view?

KAUTSKI: If you want to produce a race of plumbers, certainly.

But there was a country once: full of the whirring of doves' wings, with the thrill of marble from sea to sea, dream and ecstasy ...

RÖNNE: ... Brains, soft and rounded; dull and white.

A rosy flush spreading and rustling groves of blue.

Forehead soft and blooming. All tension eased in yearning towards shores.

The banks piled high with oleander, then lost to view in fragrant, gentle bays.

... Blood now seems ready to burst. Temples to surge with hope.

In my forehead, the coursing of waters about to take flight.

Oh, the rush of ecstasy like a dove to my heart: laughing, laughing—

Ithaca!—Ithaca! ...

Oh stay! stay! Don't send me back! Such a path to tread, homewards at last, as the blossom falls sweet and heavy from all the worlds ... (*Goes up to the professor and takes hold of him.*)

PROFESSOR: Gentlemen, what are you trying to do? I am more than willing to meet your wishes. You have my assurance that in future I shall invariably give out in my lectures that we in this faculty cannot teach ultimate wisdom and that lectures in philosophy should be followed at the same time. I shall not fail to emphasise that the nature of our knowledge is open to question ...

(*Shouting.*) Listen to me, gentlemen! After all, we are all scientists, we must avoid fantasy. Why should we get involved in situations which the structure of modern society is—let's say—not equipped to cope with ... We are doctors after all, don't let us overdo questions of belief. No one will ever know what took place here!

Murder! Murder!

LUTZ: (*Also taking hold of him.*) Murder! Murder! Fetch some shovels. Back to the ground with this lump of clay! Lash this scum with our foreheads!

PROFESSOR: (*Choking.*) You callow youths! You murky dawn! Your life blood will be shed and the mob will feast in triumph over it! Go on, trample the north under foot! Logic

will triumph! On every side the same abyss: Ignorabimus!
Ignorabimus!

LUTZ: (*Smashing him repeatedly with his forehead.*)
Ignorabimus! Take that for your ignorabimus! Your
researches weren't deep enough! Go deeper into things if you
want to teach us! We are the young generation. Our blood
cries out for the heavens and the earth and not for cells and
invertebrates. Yes, we're trampling the north underfoot. The
hills of the south are swelling up already. Oh soul, open wide
your wings; soul! soul! We must have Dream. We must have
Ecstasy. Our cry is Dionysos and Ithaca!

BRAINS (1914)

'If words can be said to lie, it might be thought that
they were doing so here.'

Rönne, a young doctor, whose main occupation at one time
had been dissecting, was passing through southern Germany
on his way north. He had done nothing for some months
now; for two years he had held a post in an institute of
pathology—that is to say, approximately two thousand bodies
had passed through his unthinking hands and for some reason
this had left him strangely exhausted.

Now he was sitting in his corner seat taking note of his
journey; through vine-growing country, he remarked to himself, fairly flat, past scarlet fields on fire with poppies. It's not
too hot, blue is streaming across the sky, a humid blue wafted
skywards from lakeshores; every house is propped up by roses,
one or two quite smothered by them.

I must buy a note-book and a pencil; I must take down
everything I can from now on so that things don't flash past
out of sight. So many years to my life, and it's all sunk
without trace. When I was starting out, did things stick? I
can't remember.

Then tunnel after tunnel and his eyes strained to catch the
light again; men out working in the hay; wooden bridges,
stone bridges; a town and a car on the mountain-side in front
of a house.

Verandahs, wards and coachhouses, on top of a mountain,

built into a wood—this was where Rönne was to be locum to the doctor in charge for a few weeks. The power of Life is so great, he thought, this hand will never be able to undermine it and he looked at his right hand.

The only people in the hospital precinct were employees and patients; the hospital was high up; Rönne's mood was solemn; as he discussed professional matters with the nurses his tone was distant and cool and his loneliness shone from him like a halo.

He left it to them—turning the handle, fixing the lamps, starting the motors, focusing light on this or that with the help of a mirror; he took comfort in seeing science broken down into a series of manipulations, some calling for the brute strength of a blacksmith, others the delicacy of a watchmaker.

Then he took his hands, passed them over the X-ray tube, adjusted the mercury of the quartz lamp, increased or decreased the gap through which light fell on to a back, inserted a funnel into an ear, took cotton-wool, placed it in the ear-duct, and was at once absorbed in the consequences of this operation in the owner of the ear—he watched how concepts took shape, concepts of helper, healing, good doctor, of universal trust and joy in life, and he observed how the draining off of fluids acquired spiritual overtones. Next came a casualty, and he took a small board, padded with cotton-wool, placed it beneath the injured finger, tied a starched bandage round it and reflected that this finger had been broken by jumping over a ditch or by an unseen root, through high spirits or carelessness, in short, in what close conjunction with the course of this life and its contingencies; and yet he had to care for it like someone remote, out of reach, and he listened for the voice, far away in the depths, which came at the moment when the pain started.

It was the usual hospital practice with hopeless cases to conceal the true facts and send them back to their families, because of the paperwork and mess death brings with it. Rönne went up to one such case and examined him: the frontal orifice, the back covered with sores, and in between some crumbling flesh; he congratulated the man on his successful cure and watched him trotting off out of sight. He will go home how, thought Rönne, take the pains for an unpleasant side-effect of recovery, commit himself to the idea of a new life, he will educate his son, see to the upbringing of his daughter, live up to the rôle of honest citizen, to the universal concept of good neighbour till the night comes and the blood in his throat. If words can ever be said to lie, then surely they do so here. But if I could lie with words then presumably I should not be here. Everywhere I look words are a condition of life. If only I had been lying when I said to him, Good luck!

One morning he sat at his breakfast table utterly shaken. The feeling in him was so strong: the doctor in charge would go off, about this time a locum would come, get up and have breakfast; one thinks and one eats and one's breakfast does its work. But still he continued to ask such questions and issue such orders as the performance of his duties required; he tapped a finger of his right hand against a finger of his left and there was a lung underneath; he went up to beds—good morning, how do you feel? But now from time to time it could happen on his way through the wards that he failed to put the routine question to every patient—about the frequency of his coughs or his rectal temperature-reading. When I am on my rounds—this preoccupied him abnormally—I am swallowed up by one pair of eyes after another, I am observed and weighed up. I am associated with friendly objects and solemn ones: sometimes I merge with a house where they long to be, sometimes with a stick of liquorice they once enjoyed. And once I too had a pair of eyes, always looking backwards; yes, indeed; I existed, incurious and composed. What have I come to? Where am I? A gentle fluttering, a breeze blowing past.

He tried to think when it had all begun, but he had no idea any more; as I walk down a street I see a house and remember a palace in Florence that looked similar, but the flash of resemblance fades at once.

Something is weakening me from above. There is nothing solid behind my eyes any more. On all sides space surges off into infinity; once surely it flowed together at one spot. The cortex that was holding me up has crumbled.

Often when he got back to his room from one of these rounds he would twist his hands this way and that and look at them. And once a nurse observed him smelling them or rather going over them as though testing their atmosphere, and she watched him putting his lightly cupped hands together, little finger to little finger, then pressing them open and shut, as though squeezing open the halves of a large, soft fruit or bending something in two. She told the other nurses but no one knew what it might mean. Till the day when an animal of larger than usual size was being slaughtered in the hospital. Rönne came along, apparently by chance, just as the head was being split open, took the contents in both hands and forced the two halves apart. In a flash the nurse realised that this was the gesture she had witnessed in the corridor. But she could see no connection between this and anything else and soon forgot about it.

But Rönne went for walks in the gardens. It was summertime—the blue of the sky danced in the viper's bugloss, roses were in bloom, their heads fragrant. He could feel the upsurge of life in the earth; stopping short of his feet, and the welling of natural forces: no longer entering his blood. In the main, however, he took paths which lay in the shade and had plenty of seats; he had to rest frequently from the remorseless glare and he felt at the mercy of a breathless sky.

By degrees he began to be irregular in the performance of his duties; in particular, in conversation with the bursar or the matron when he had to express an opinion about something, when he had the feeling that now was the moment to contribute his considered opinion on a particular topic he went to pieces completely. What can one possibly say of something that has happened? Had it not happened that way, it would have happened a little differently. Its place would never stay empty. All he wished to do was gaze gently into space and lie down in his room.

But when he was here he did not lie like a person who had arrived only a few weeks before from a lakeside far over the mountains; he looked rather as though he had grown there along with the place where his body now lay and been weakened by the long years of lying; and there was something stiff and waxen about him, possibly derived from the bodies with which he had been associated.

And he continued to be preoccupied with his hands. The nurse who looked after him loved him dearly, he always spoke so pleadingly to her, though she had little idea what about. He often began rather scornfully, saying that he knew these strange structures, for he had held them in his hands. But straightaway he would go off again—they were ruled by laws not made by Man, their fate was as foreign to us as that of a river on which we happen to be sailing. And then he gave way completely, his eyes already in darkness: it was a question of twelve chemical substances which had combined without awaiting his command and which would separate again without consulting him. If so, what was one to speak to? One's words just drifted over them.

There was no longer any reality facing him; he had lost all power over space, he said once; he stayed lying down almost all the time scarcely moving.

He locked himself into his room so that no one could burst in on him; he wanted to open it and confront whoever came, coolly.

He gave instructions for hospital cars to drive up and down on the road outside; he had noticed that the sound of their wheels soothed him; it was so distant, it was like long ago, it belonged to a city far away.

He always lay in the same position: stiff on his back. He lay on his back in a reclining chair, the chair was in a square room, the room was in a house and the house was on a hill. Apart from a few birds he was the most advanced species. And so the earth bore him gently and smoothly through the ether and past all the stars.

One evening he went down to the verandahs; he looked along the rows of deck chairs with their occupants lying quietly under their covers awaiting recovery; he looked at them lying there—each with a home-town, each a creature of dream-filled sleep, of evening homecoming, of songs passed on from father to son, poised between happiness and death. He looked along the verandah and went back.

The doctor in charge was recalled, he was a friendly person, he said that one of his daughters had fallen ill. But Rönne said, Look, I held them in these hands of mine, a hundred, maybe even a thousand of them; some soft, some hard, all ready to dissolve; men, women, with crumbling flesh and full of blood. But now I am holding my own in my hands and I can't stop probing into the limits of my possibilities. Supposing the forceps had pressed a little harder here when I was born? Supposing I had been struck on the head again and again on the same spot? What is it about brains? I always wanted to float free in the air like a bird soaring up out of a ravine; yet I am still apart, walled in by crystal. Please now, let me through, I am taking flight once more—I have been so weary—I am borne aloft by wings— with my sword of blue anemones—in the falling rays of the mid-day sun—in ruins of the south—crumbling cloudbanks— skulls turning to dust—foreheads collapsing at the temple.

ADDRESS TO HEINRICH MANN

Nihilism is a feeling of pleasure

I shall come straight to the central point, which the phenomenon of Heinrich Mann and his work seem to me to raise for our age, and I shall attempt to discuss this one point. You will find this point most clearly presented and most excitingly developed in his famous essay on Flaubert and George Sand... Strike out their names over this essay, replace them with the title 'art' and you have the theme of the essay which is really nothing more nor less than one great dramatic monologue by Heinrich Mann on himself and the driving forces within him: Flaubert's name may be attached to those pages... but they are really concerned with the man who picked up the spear where Flaubert laid it down, and introduced another race, and a completely different age to the phenomenon of art.

He brought art to Germany, art to our time. Art, in Germany always before its time, nowadays even as Thomas Mann said in a recent speech, something which many people would place practically in the criminal category. Art, for the German of the last century applicable by common acceptance only to music, the German, that fool of this earth, as Hebbel called him, that Adam in chains in the animal kingdom. Art in Germany, always exclusively eighteenth century: inferior to real scientific knowledge, grade two means of cognition, base view of pure concept in physical terms. Here there is no appreciation of forms, contours, plasticity, here everything has

85

to be fluid: ... the hippopotamus philosophy, Heraclitus the first German, Plato the second German, Hegelians to a man, even if there had never been a Hegel, you know about the extensive parallels between the Hellenic and the German spirit, all of us exist only through this inter-dependence: the only difference being that we never won the battle the Greeks did, the marble victory over the Aegean Sea to the East.

In Germany education was widespread in the guise of art, poetry which tended to be good for one, humanistic ideals which the nineteenth century had put all its weight behind with all the intellectual and social consequences; this meant Heyse and Dahn; this meant Ranke and Haeckel; this meant art and science as the bloom of periclean prosperity. Then around 1900 the Mann brothers came on the scene and cast a phosphorescent glow. They taught a literary generation the danger, the intoxication, the decay which is notoriously part and parcel of things artistic— ... brought with them art as the high spiritual corruption, to feel what had never been felt before, brought with them refinements still to be discovered, brought with them—your minds are ready for the word— artistry (*Artistik*), a phenomenon never more to be extinguished for Germany. As far as this country was concerned they had only one ancestor, but he was mentally broken and did not count: *Nietzsche*: delicacy in all five artistic senses, intuition for nuances, psychological morbidity, gravity in the mise en scene, that Parisian gravity par excellence, the artist's gospel: 'art as the real task for life, art as life's metaphysical fulfilment'. That's what we find in his theory—and its realisation in the work of art some decades later in the manner of him whom we celebrate today.

The artistic invasion, the new art! From the west, intellect: fanaticism of expression, analytical instinct, versed in harmonies and penetrating as X-rays; from the north the eruptive quality of enormous themes, the dark tragic dreams.

Art *an sich*: I wonder, he asks in this essay we are looking at, whether a book cannot produce the same effect, regardless of what it says. Isn't there, in the precision with which the words are placed, the unusualness of the component parts, the surface polish, the harmony of the whole, isn't there an *inner* virtue in that, a kind of divine power, something eternal like a principle?

86

Absolute art: Flaubert, Mann says, believed in laws of beauty which are like the Lord's commandments and preserve the eternal in what is created. Seeing some pillars of the Acropolis made him realise what lasting beauty could be attained with the arrangement of sentences, phrases, words. *In truth you see he did not believe that there is anything external in art.*

The incursion of artistry—: words, phrases! Put another way, an art without moral force, without national background, strongly intellectual, let's say it: light-weight, purely technical, and, what is more, not even trying to be entertaining? O Art, what mysteries do you hold, said Violante, but they did not see it that way in Germany. The general public still had not discerned the connection between European nihilism and dionysian form, between sceptical relativity and artistic mystery, between the inflated ecstasies and raptures of the German spirit and this superficiality based on depth, this Olympus based on pure appearance: the general public did not yet see from what waves Violante really arose, and what kind of life her white face looked out over, over what great dreams of centuries she departed.

Not yet. But doesn't the sentence from the *Will to Power* sound much more familiar nowadays? An antimetaphysical philosophy—all right, but then in that case an artistic one. Is it not in the air in the battle which the German of today is fighting, the battle for an anti-ideological philosophy, a temporal, expressive one, running counter to his metaphorical vices, his vapid vagueness. As forest echoes, might it not just be aesthetic idealism and gallic *esprit* behind this concept of artistry, but something more besides. Did perhaps Nietzsche, did perhaps the great writers we started with, see a movement developing from him which started philosophically but ended politically, possibly in the direction of a new European ethos with a new German morality in it. If the nature of the German is always to be stuck at the formative process, eternal non-present and boundless growth, repulsive inadequacy and vast hope, if this is what makes all the other peoples of this earth see him as so suspect, so unreasonable—if according to Nietzsche (all things bring a parallel) the German loves the clouds and everything unclear, gestating, lowering, damp and pre-ordained and feels that whatever is in any way uncertain, unformed, shifting, growing must be profound—couldn't *this* be the start of a counter-movement, one we have not often enough attained, not the crane's flight of the intellectual leaders over the people, but a relief movement against this terrible German feeling that man is to be found in what is devouring, insatiable, murderous, a counter-movement for order, spatial-spiritual order, hard-worn forms, shape, this-worldliness, Latinity. If the German likes to haunt corridors and secret passages, caves, hiding-holes and dungeons, always in disorder and on secret paths to chaos—if according to Hebbel the most detested among nations, if according to Goethe his is the nation which offers most scope for meanness—does not danger produce its own antidote, when the clear masters of the word reach down into their language, this language of the vatic and prophetic, masters who are both profound in the Venetian and light in the Genoan fashion, perhaps those between the races, perhaps the westerners, perhaps those on a high ridge between two seas, when they teach us to chisel a hand's breadth of prose for days like a statue, each page flawless, each sentence cool—when they counter the wide-ranging wildness of the German spirit with those moments and miracles in which a great force voluntarily stopped short of the infinite and boundless, in which in a surfeit of fine pleasure they show where order, the great law lies, by sudden restraint and petrefaction, by stopping and taking up a position on still quivering ground. Could not a nation take them as models for clarity, or the gold and cold round things that have achieved perfection, could not a nation begin to look up to this positivism of hard-won, hard and absolute things rather than looking up to that other positivism of anonymous truth, and amorphous knowledge, the fluctuating formulas of scientific relativity? In that case, Nietzsche would have said, could not a nation which had arrived at completely different perspectives, see art too in an entirely different light, art as the only real reason for living the last transcendence inside the great European nihilism, artistic, dionysian art, which is perhaps as meaningless as space and time and things thought and unthought, and that entirely from that reflection of immortality which arises out of sinking cities and crumbling empires from a vase or verse made of perfect form, inviolate and perfect—in a land thus transformed by art perhaps that poet marked out for tragedy dreamt he heard the Hölderlin question: Oh soul of the fatherland, when will you appear as a perfect whole? and his own answer ring out: that I bade you sing, my soul, that was my ultimate desire. Art as the ultimate, the new art, artistry, the post-Nietzschean epoch, wherever it reached any eminence, was arrived at as the result of the antithesis between delirium and discipline. On the one hand always the profound nihilism of all values, above this, however, the transcendence of the creative urge. To this day nothing has taken us beyond this point, no political, mythic, racial, or collective ideology. Our eye is still caught by the thrill of the *Ecce homo* feelings in Heinrich Mann's Herzogin von Assy novels. The thrilling *Ecce homo* feelings: *nihilism is a feeling of delight* and in the intellect man has a marvellous means of self-destruction: the art of the Herzogin von Assy: as inclination and method, mystery and monomania, see on this point the uncanny words of Flaubert: je suis mystique et je ne crois à rien. This is how I see the situation, this is how I see the century, shot through with the duchess of Assy's dreams; but when the new is to start—that I still cannot see.

TO THE LITERARY EMIGRÉS: A REPLY

You have written me a letter from somewhere near Marseilles. You say in it that the young Germans who at one time so much admired me and my books are now living as refugees in small Mediterranean resorts on the Gulf of Lyons and in hotel rooms in Zürich, Prague and Paris. You have heard from newspaper reports, you explain, that I have offered my services to the new State, that I have come out publicly in support of it, that as a member of the Academy I have not dissented from its cultural plans. You request a personal statement from me—a request which is friendly, if extremely pointed. You write: what has persuaded you—you, whose name was synonymous for us with the highest intellectual standards and a purity little short of fanatical—to offer your services to people whom the rest of Europe finds lacking in those very qualities? What are the new friends like compared with the old ones you are about to lose? Who will understand you there? You will always remain the intellectual, that is an object of suspicion, and no one will want to know you. You request a statement, you warn me, you demand an unequivocal answer. 'He who will not declare himself for us in this hour, must henceforth and for evermore depart from us.' Here, then, you have my answer which is, of course, unequivocal.

In the first place I must tell you that I have come to the conclusion, on the basis of much that has happened in recent weeks, that it is possible to discuss what is happening in Germany only with those who have personal experience, inside Germany, of these events. Only with those people who have lived through the tenseness of recent months, who have experienced it all directly and uninterruptedly from one hour to the next, from one newspaper to the next, from news bulletin to news bulletin and who have struggled day and night to come to terms with it, even with those who neither cheered nor waved flags but rather suffered it in silence, with all those one can discuss it, but with the refugees, those who went abroad, it is not possible. For the latter have missed the chance to feel welling up within them, not intellectually but as part of themselves, not in the abstract but as a powerful natural impulse, the concept which is so foreign to them of 'Volk', they have missed the chance to experience the phenomenon of 'national' oneness—an epithet used once again, in your letter, to such arrogant and condescending effect—in its true force, in accents of genuine conviction, they have missed the chance to watch history at work—a history rich in forms and images, possibly tragic, unquestionably decreed by fate. I am not referring here to the theatricality of these events, the impressionist-like magic of torchlight processions and music, but to the inner process, the release of massive creative energy, which brought about a far-reaching human transformation even in an onlooker who originally had been an opponent.

For this reason alone we are not likely to reach agreement. But this possibility is ruled out in any case by another problem which for years has come between your friends and myself on a theoretical level, but which has now suddenly become startlingly immediate, so much so that each one of us is forced to take now a deliberate binding decision. The best way to approach this problem is to consider the word 'barbarism', which appears repeatedly in your letter as well as in other communications I have received. You make it seem as though what is now happening in Germany were a threat to culture and civilisation, as though a horde of savages were threatening the ideals of humanity as a whole, but—and this is the question I put to you in return—how do you really visualise the process of history? Do you imagine it to be particularly active in French seaside resorts? What do you think, for instance, that the twelfth century was like, the transition from the Romanesque to the Gothic sensibility, do you imagine this was 'arrived at after discussion'? Do you imagine that someone, in the north of that same country from whose southern region you now write, 'thought out' a new architectural style? That there was a 'vote'—rounded arches or pointed, or a 'debate' on apses—rounded or polygonal? I think you would do much better to give up this novelettish view of history and see it instead as something elemental, thrusting, inescapable; I think you would get a truer picture of events in Germany if you could stop seeing history as the balance-sheet presented to creation by your nineteenth-century bourgeois minds—no, history owes you nothing, on the contrary, and it has never heard of your democracy or of the rationalism which you still maintain, though perhaps with an effort; the only method, the only style of operating known to history is to bring forth at its turning points, from the inexhaustible fertility of the human race, a new type of Man who must fight his way through, who must force the message of his generation and his kind on the age he lives in, not by yielding, but by action and suffering, as the law of Life decrees. Naturally, this view of history is neither enlightened nor humanitarian but metaphysical—so, too, to an even greater degree is my conception of Man. And so we have arrived at the crux of our longstanding disagreement—namely, your charge that I am fighting for an irrational principle.

The relevant passage in your letter runs as follows: 'Come out in support of the Irrational as the first step, then it'll be barbarism, in a flash it's Adolf Hitler'. You write these words at a point in history when, in full view of everyone your opportunistic, progressive conception of Man has utterly failed over large tracts of the globe, when it has become clear, on the one hand that this was a superficial, irresponsible and hedonistic view, and on the other that in none of the truly great epochs of human history has the nature of Man been regarded as other than irrational—that is to say, close to the creative process and capable of creation. Please get it into your heads as you sit far away by your Latin sea that these events in Germany are not simply politicians up to their tricks which can then be given the full dialectical treatment and totally distorted. What is taking place is the emergence of a new biological type, a change of direction in history, the coming of a new national stock. It is undeniable that this last idea rests on a conception of human nature according to which Man may or may not be rational, but above all is mythical and profound. Undeniably, the view taken of his future is that it must be grafted on to a distant stage in the history of the race, for Man is older than the French Revolution believed and more complex than the Enlightenment thought. Undeniably, one's instinct is that Man is part of Nature, close to the creative process, it has become a fact of experience that he is much less detached, much more vulnerably involved in Life than the mere two thousand years of prattle about the antithesis of ideal and reality would make us believe. In fact he is eternal Pleistocene, a barbarian menagerie with a cultural overlay even since the end of the Ice Age: diluvial web of temperament, Cainozoic *bric à brac*; in fact he is eternal, primordial vision; waking, daytime, reality; a loose agglomeration of rhythms hammered out by hidden creative frenzies. If only you would understand, you amateurs of civilisation and troubadours of western progress, that it is not a question of governmental structures, but of a new vision of the birth of Man—as a conception it may be old or it may perhaps be the last magnificent product of the white race, probably one of the world spirit's most magnificent creations in our time, adumbrated in the Goethe hymn, To Nature; and if only you would grasp the further fact that this vision is not subject to success or failure, if ten wars in East and West were to overwhelm and annihilate the German people, if the Apocalypse were approaching by land and sea with its seals about to be broken, this vision of humanity would still stand: in order to realise it, the nation must be bred and your philological inquiry about civilisation and barbarism is shown up as absurd in the face of an over-whelming historical reality.

But let us leave philosophy and pass on to politics, let us turn aside from the vision and confront the facts of experience. There you are in your seaside resorts demanding statements from us because we are collaborating in the construction of a new state whose faith is remarkable, whose seriousness of purpose is extraordinary, and whose situation, both internally and externally, is so grave that it would need Iliads and Aeneids to tell of its fate. Before the eyes of the rest of the world you wish war on this state and this nation, a war of annihilation, total collapse, death. It is the nation whose name you bear, whose language you speak, whose schools you attended, whose scientific and artistic traditions form your entire intellectual heritage, whose industry printed your books, whose theatres put on your plays, who gave you fame and renown, whose inhabitants you wish to have for your readers in as large numbers as possible and who even now would have interfered with you very little, had you but stayed. There you sit gazing out across the sea which stretches away to Africa—perhaps at this moment a warship is under way full of negro troops, some of the 600,000 colonial soldiers of the notorious French *forces d'outremer* destined to attack Germany and perhaps the Arc de Triomphe or the Hradschin as well, and you swear vengeance on this country whose only political objective is to secure its own future, this country from which most of you intellectually have received much, to which you have given nothing. You state in your letter that you have only now, but now in the fullest sense of the word, become true Marxists, that taunts of 'vulgar Marxists' or 'materialism' will not stop you from fighting our 'hysterical brutality', your position is on the side of the spirit—you are joining forces with it in the war against 'political reaction'. I have no idea what these phrases are meant to mean, they seem to me to belong to an era light years away, I could after all put the question to you—did you refer to hysterical brutality when the state where your Marxism is triumphant put to death two million bourgeois intellectuals? But I shall assume that you mean Socialism and the most notable of the German intellectuals living abroad have indeed in recent years often spoken out on behalf of the rights of the German

93

workers, most honourably and publicly and repeatedly Thomas Mann. I would inform these people that the German worker today is better off than ever before. You are aware that as a doctor I come into contact with many social groups, including through my industrial insurance work many workers, including, too, many who used to be Communists and members of the German Socialist Party without any doubt at all, so they all tell me, they are better off than they ever were. They are better treated at work, supervisory staffs are more cautious, personnel staff more polite, the workers have more power, they get more respect, morale at work is higher thanks to a new awareness of their political rôle, and what the Socialist party was unable to win for them they have been given by this new form of Socialism, namely, a motivating sense of life. You must accept that the new holders of power will continue to win the workers over: the sense of the community of a whole people in Germany is no empty sham and the First of May was no shady capitalist trick, it was truly impressive, wholly genuine: work suddenly lost the stigma of a yoke, it is no longer, as it has been in recent decades, the suffering sent to punish the proletariat—it was revealed as the foundation of a newly forming community marked by the dissolution of the class-system; there can be no doubt, for anyone who was there to see, that this year of 1933 has in many ways given a new, clearly defined shape to the varieties of European socialism which have been in the air for decades—it has proclaimed a new section of the Declaration of Human Rights. So if in using the phrase 'political reaction' you meant that you wish to fight for workers' rights, you should join the new state, not slander it.

But your letter is also directed at me personally. You put your questions—some in warning, some in interrogation—about the special nature of my radical views on language, views which would earn me mockery and contempt on the other side, and also about my admiration of certain literary names who are now, you say, on *your* side. My reply is this: I shall continue to revere what I have always held to be exemplary and instructive for German literature, I shall revere it right down to Lugano and beyond to the Ligurian Sea, but my personal commitment is to the new state because it is my people who are making themselves a new destiny. What right have I to opt out—do I know any better way—no! I can try so far as lies in my power to guide it onwards to the point of my choice, but even were I to fail, it would remain my people, my Volk. A wealth of meaning in that word—Volk! I owe my spiritual and economic existence, my language, my life, my personal relationships, the sum total of my brain, above all to my people. From it came my ancestors, to it my children will return. And since I grew up in the country, in the midst of flocks, I also know the meaning of 'homeland'. The city, industry, intellectualism, all shadows cast on my thoughts by the age we live in, all an expression of the twentieth century to which in my writings I am subject, there are moments when this whole tortured existence fades away and there is nothing left but the plain, vastness, seasons, the soil, simple words: *Volk*. That is why I come to offer my services to those whom Europe, according to your letter, despises. Europe! With its precious values—where it has to make do without bribes and guns, it cuts a pretty miserable figure! Just now it is whispering in your ear that the 'Volk' is not behind Hitler, but only his 'sheep'—as Lady Oxford wrote recently in the *News Chronicle*. A great mistake! It is the '*Volk*'! Just compare those great men, Hitler and Napoleon. No question but Napoleon was greater as an individual genius. There was nothing impelling the whole French nation to conquer the pyramids and to send its armies all over Europe, nothing but the one mighty military genius. In Germany today you constantly hear people asking: which came first, Hitler or the movement? The question is revealing, one cannot tell simply because the two are identical. It really is a case of the magical coincidence of the individual and the general which Burckhardt refers to in his *Reflections on History,* in his description of great men from the course of world history. Great men—it is all there—the perils at the outset, their appearance almost always in terrifying times, the incredible perseverance, the extraordinary facility in everything, not least the organic functions, and then too the suspicion growing in all thinking people that this is the man to achieve what only he can do and yet what must be done. Note carefully that I said 'all thinking people' and you know that I set thought above everything else. I have always used a saying of Hegel's to test my political instinct: that form of

95

higher obstinacy which consists in refusing to acknowledge in one's outlook anything that is not sanctioned by one's thoughts is a credit to Mankind. I ask you therefore to believe me and not to deceive yourselves. Whatever Europe may whisper in your ear: the whole Volk is behind this movement, peace-loving and hardworking but if need be willing to die.

Finally, a topic on which you, living abroad, once you have read the preceding paragraphs, will certainly want precise information: I am not a Party member, am not in touch with its leaders, I do not expect to find new friends. I am impelled to write this by my fanatical purity, of which you write in such flattering terms, my purity of thought and feeling. The foundations of these views are shared by every thinker in history. One said: the seeds of happiness are not sown in the soil of world history (Fichte); another: nations have a duty to realise what is greatest and most vital in themselves regardless of the good of the individual or the greatest good of the greatest number (Burckhardt); a third: the increasingly reduced scale of Man's existence is the most urgent possible reason to breed a stronger race. Also: a masterful race can arise only from fearful and violent beginnings. Problem—where are the barbarians of the twentieth century? (Nietzsche). All of this had been completely forgotten by the era of liberalism and individualism which, in any case, had not the intellectual capacity to accept it as a challenge and to follow through its political consequences. Then suddenly dangers loom, suddenly the community finds a new compactness and each and every citizen, including the man of letters, must come forward and take his stand: as amateur, in private or as supporter of the State. My choice is the latter and I must accept it in the name of the State when you bid me farewell from your distant shore.

CONFESSION OF FAITH IN EXPRESSIONISM

At a great political rally which took place recently in the Berlin Sports Palace, one which was particularly exhaustively covered by the press, the custodian of the Rhineland folk galleries addressed himself to the question of Expressionism. He described Expressionism in painting as debased, anarchistic and snobbish, he called Expressionism in music cultural Bolshevism and summed the whole thing up as a mockery of the people. As it happens, Expressionism in literature is at the same time also being publicly condemned yet again: a famous German writer feels no qualms about stating that this generation was made up of deserters, convicts and crooks, that they had inflated the value of their wares with enormous sensations like crooked brokers pushing a phoney investment; he describes it as being totally unprincipled in looseness of living, and he names names, among them mine.

And in fact I am listed in several histories of literature, for example in Soergel's *Under the Expressionist Spell*, as one of the founders of German literary Expressionism along with Heym, and I admit that psychologically I move within its orbit and feel its method (about which I shall speak in a moment) to be the one that comes naturally to me; this being so, and as in addition I am the only one of this dispersed group who has the honour to be a member of the new German Academy of Literature, I shall speak on behalf of this group. Defend its name, awaken the memory of its inner situation and point out certain things in its defence, in defence of a generation whose first flower was destroyed by the war, in which many died: Stramm, Stadler, Lichtenstein, Trakl, Marc, Macke, Rudi Stephan; and whose minds bore enormous existential burdens, the burdens of the last generation of a world largely doomed to destruction.

I

First of all, one point must be put straight—Expressionism was no German frivolity, neither was it some foreign fabrication; it was a European style. In Europe between 1910 and 1925 there was no naïve, that is to say object-directed, art any more, there was only anti-naturalistic art. Picasso is Spanish; Léger and Braque, French; Carra and Chirico, Italian; Archipenko and Kandinsky, Russian; Masereel, Flemish; Brancusi, Roumanian; Kokoschka, Austrian; Klee, Hofer, Belling, Poelzig, Gropius, Kirchner and Schmitt-Rotluff, German; every country in Europe is represented and every single one is an Aryan. In music Stravinsky is Russian; Bartók is Hungarian; Malipiero, Italian; Alban Berg and

Krenek, Austrian; Honegger, Swiss; Hindemith, German, and all of them are European. In literature Heym, Stramm, Georg Kaiser, Edschmid, Wedekind, Sorge, Sack, Goering, Johannes R. Becher, Däubler, Stadler, Trakl, Loerke, Brecht are pure German. Incidentally Hanns Johst also developed out of this great collection of talent. So we have before us a great closed front of artists of exclusively European descent. The outbreak of a new style on such a broad front speaks without further explanation for the completely autochthonous, elemental nature of its forms, for a new natural state of the European family. Similarly it can not in any way be explained away as reaction against preceding styles—Naturalism or Impressionism: it is simply a new historical state. A state which, from the formal as well as the human point of view, was of decidedly revolutionary character, as Marinetti declared in his fundamental manifesto of 1909 'The Love of Danger', 'Getting used to Power and Daring', 'The Point of Attack', 'The Death Leap', 'The Lovely Idea one dies for'. Incidentally Fascism took up this movement, Marinetti is today an ambassador and president of the Roman Academy of Arts. It is not quite correct to say it was taken up: Futurism helped to create Fascism; the black shirt, the battle cry and song of battle Giovinezza derive from Arditismo, the warlike section of Futurism.

Futurism as a style, also called Cubism, and in Germany generally described as Expressionism, assumed many shapes in its empirical transformations, but was undivided in its basic inner position of destruction of reality, its ruthless way of going to the root of things, to the point where they can no longer be individually or sensually coloured, falsified, softened or pushed into the psychological process to be exploited, but instead in the acausal infinite silence of the absolute ego await the rare call from the creative spirit—this style had already been foreshadowed throughout the nineteenth century. There are many passages in Goethe, which are pure Expressionism, e.g. verses like the famous 'toothless jaws chatter and the tottering limbs, he enraptured by the last ray', etc., in which there is absolutely no connection between the various parts as far as content is concerned, only in the manner of expression; no one theme is presented consistently, instead inner excitements, magically compulsive associations of a purely transcendental kind make the link. There is a vast number of such passages in *Faust II,* and many throughout the work of the older Goethe. The same is true of Kleist: *Penthesilea* is a dramatically pure verse orgy of excitement. Then we find it in Nietzsche, his (and equally Hölderlin's) fragmentary poetry is pure Expressionism: super-charging of the word, of few words with an enormous accumulation of creative tension, better perhaps 'ein Ergreifen von Worten aus Spannung' and these totally mystically apprehended words then live on with a genuinely inexplicable power of suggestion. In modern literature rich seams of expressive writing can be shown in Carl Hauptmann; and in Paul Fechter's history of literature, which is not at all well-disposed to Expressionism, we find the interesting reminder of Hermann Conradi (1862-90), in whom Fechter sees early indications of Joyce, Proust and Jahnn, and even Freud; in Conradi analysis is an end in itself, says Fechter; he penetrates to the 'inner reality'. This inner reality and its rise straight into formal combinations is exactly the kind of art we are talking about: in musical composition we find it already in Richard Wagner's passages of absolute music, his 'flight into primeval states', as Nietzsche called it. In painting Cézanne (France), Van Gogh (Holland), Munch (Norway), are fore-runners and at the same time masters of this style. So we are justified in saying that there is an expressionistic ingredient in all art, and that only at one particular time, namely in the decade immediately past, did it emerge from many minds as the representative style of the age.

II

I have said that in Europe between 1910 and 1925 there was practically no style which was not anti-naturalistic; there was also practically no reality, at most there was only the mask of reality. Reality was a capitalistic concept, Reality meant real estate, industrial goods, mortgages, everything which could be reckoned in terms of price with profit for the middle-man. Reality meant Darwinism, international steeple-chases, and everything else in any way privileged. Reality in those days meant war, starvation, the humiliations of history, disenfranchisement, power. The mind had no reality. It turned instead to its inner reality, its being, its biology, its structure, its cross-fertilisations of physiological and psychological nature, its creativeness, its radiance. The way to experience this, to ensure its possession, was to heighten its productive element, something Indian, namely ecstasy, a definite form of inner trance. But from an ethnological point of view there is nothing wrong with ecstasies. Dionysius descended upon the sober pastoral people and these by no means hysterical mountain clans staggered after him in orphic procession, and later Meister Eckhart and Jakob Böhme had visions too. Elemental encounter with rapture! Naturally there was also Schiller, Bach, Dürer, these natural assets, nourishing sources, life streams, but they were fundamentally different, but it was nature, that of 1910-25, it was even more than nature, it was identity between mind and time.

Reality—Europe's demonic concept: happy alone the ages and generations, in which there was an unquestioned reality, remembering the first deep tremor in the Middle Ages at the crumbling of religious reality, and the fundamental collapse since 1900 with the disintegration of scientific reality, which had been the source of what was 'real' for the last 400 years. New reality—science apparently being capable only of destroying the old—could be discerned only by looking inwards and backwards. Outside, all the old remnants were falling apart, leaving in their place only relationships and functions; random, rootless Utopias; humanitarian, social or pacifistic scraps of paper, governed by an abstract process, an abstract economic force; sense or goal was illusory, formless, ideological, but in the foreground everywhere sat a flora and fauna of managerial monads and all hid behind functions and abstracts. Dissolution of nature, dissolution of history. The old realities space and time: functions of formulae; sickness and health; functions of consciousness; even the most concrete forces like state and society were substantially beyond anyone's grasp, there was always just the operation in itself, always just the process as such—: striking aphorism by Ford, equally brilliant whether as philosophy or business maxim: first create the cars, then the roads will follow: that's to say, first rouse the demand, then the demand will see to it that it is satisfied; first start the process, then it will run on of its own accord—and it did, brilliant psychology of the white race: impoverished but maniacal; undernourished, but jubilant; with twenty marks in their back pocket they look down on Sils-Maria and Golgotha and buy formulae in the functional process. That was 1920-25, that was the doomed world, business, that was functionalism, ripe for the storm which came; but before that there was this handful of Expressionists, these believers in a new reality and an old absolute and with incomparable fervour, with the asceticism of saints, and the dead certainty of suffering starvation and ridicule, they tried to stop the rot with their lives.

III

Europe's last great artistic upheaval, last creative tension so fateful that a style of its own emerged from the struggle, how remarkable in view of this the rejection with which it is met today! Basically this Expressionism was the unconditional, the anti-liberal function of the spirit, at a time when the novelists, so-called epic writers, were offering the German public enormous tomes full of the most antiquated psychology and the most wretched bourgeois philosophy, when hit composers and cabaret comics in their bars and dives were producing the lousiest rhyming wit. Here at least there was conflict, clear historical law. The question with which Kant 150 years earlier had ended one philosophical epoch and started another: How is experience of the real world possible? was here taken up in the aesthetic sphere as: How is form possible? Form was no artistic concept, on the contrary it meant: what a puzzle, what a mystery, that man makes art, that he needs art, what a unique experience midst the nihilism of Europe! That was anything but intellectualism and anything but destructive. As a question it did, it is true, belong among the compulsions of the twentieth century, namely the tendency to make the unconscious conscious, to grasp experience scientifically, emotion intellectually, soul psychologically and love as a neurosis . . .

But the question was genuine readiness, genuine experience of a new being, radical and profound, and in Expressionism it brought about the only intellectual feat to leave this miserable circle of liberal opportunism, put the pure utilitarian world of science behind it, broke through the world of big business and took that difficult inward path to the creative strata, to the primal images, the myths; and in the midst of this ghastly chaos of crumbling reality and inversion of values struggled legitimately and with serious means for a new image of man. It is easy nowadays to describe this as abnormal and destructive and foreign to the people, now that the great national movement is at work creating new realities, putting new concentrations, new layers of substance in the totally defunct layers and which clearly has the moral hardness to lay a foundation on which a new art can arise. But we are talking of a time when this was not yet there, all was emptiness, when not the spirit of God but nihilism hovered over the waters, where Nietzsche's phrase applied to a whole generation of Germans: that art was the only metaphysical activity to which life still obligated us.

Art, that enormous problem! For generations European humanity had been art-orientated, had used art as its yardstick, consciously or instinctively checked all cultural, legal, phenomenological principles again and again against its mysterious basis, its manifold and impenetrable nature, and now all of a sudden it had to be for the people in all its manifestations, without regard to the state of the people, whether blooming or withering, at absolute peace or tempestuous times? The fact that a national and anthropological loss of capital had taken place, which made submission to the material of earlier periods absolutely impossible, was completely overlooked and instead art which sought its material in its own inner being was attacked simply as abnormal and foreign to the national interest. The elemental, astonishingly rigorous quality of this dazzling style was also overlooked, instead the difficulties which it doubtless presented were brushed aside simply by repeating over and over: that is purely subjective, incomprehensible, and above all, again and again: 'purely formalistic'. These criticisms are extremely paradoxical in the mouths of people who made so much of modern physics, publicly inflated it into such a bloated bastard that the newspaper reader expected the atom to be split every time he looked at a paper. This monstrous science in which there is nothing but non-concrete concepts, artificially abstracted formulae, the whole of what Goethe called a completely senseless, fabricated world. In physics theories, understood by about eight specialists in the whole world and discounted by five of these, have country houses, observatories, and Indian temples devoted exclusively to them; but if a poet concentrates on his own linguistic experience, that can only be anarchic, formalistic, even a mockery of the people. Clearly art floats freely in the air, flutters down like a snowflake, thaws out, comes to earth completely outside of time and its pressures and cultural and intellectual framework; snobbish enemies of the national interest go about their arrogant rubbish. Clearly art which does not cost anybody anything is only permitted to include what has been current in the primary schools for the last twenty years, while scientists who cost the State, the counties, the public, the tax-payers, huge sums are permitted to pump out their specialist humbug till they reach their old age pensions, all the time enjoying secure salaries, and special benefit pensions. The new Germany will certainly not commit such a stupid mistake, its leaders are themselves such artistically productive people who know too much about art, about the hybrid character of all attempts at synthesis, not to know that art has a specialist side, that this specialist side has to show itself particularly at certain critical times, and that the path of art to the people cannot always be the direct one of an immediate acceptance of the general public's vision. Actually nobody, not even the person who fails to see anything aesthetically positive in Expressionism, could deny its identity with its time, which has produced indisputable achievements and a truly national style: it was the complete parallel in aesthetic terms to modern physics and its abstract interpretations of the world, the expressive parallel to non-euclidean mathematics, which abandoned the classical concept of the last 2,000 years in favour of abstract spatial dimensions.

IV

. . . I am sure, and I see and hear it from others, that all the real Expressionists, who are now about my age, have had the same experience as I have: that, especially with their chaotic past and personal disposition, they found themselves inwardly forced into a development such as not every generation experiences, a development towards new ties and a new historical sense. Out of that unbridled, violent and delirious state that was in us, and that we exhausted, form and discipline come forward into the present day as a compulsion of quite special force. The Expressionist, more than anybody, knew the profound, technical mastery that art demands, its craft ethos, the moral of form. He was disciplined because he was the most dislocated of them all; and none of them, painter, musician or poet, would like to see a different end to the myth in which Dionysius ends up at peace, at the feet of the clear Delphic God.

So Expressionism was art, the last art of Europe, its last ray, while all around the great, long, ravaged age was dying. The epoch with art, gone for ever! The earliest Greeks had no art, they had sacral and political stone carvings, commissioned odes, ritual arrangements: art starts with Aeschylus, then there are 2,000 art-orientated years, now it is all over again. What is beginning now, what is starting now, won't be art, it is more, it is less . . .

v

One criticism levelled against this last generation certainly goes to the heart of the matter and is completely justified: it had not assumed any historic patriotic mission, it had lived the last years pretty well without any political instinct, but this almost totally apolitical nature was after all something indigenous to Germany, Goethe and Hölderlin were apolitical too, so were Rilke and George. Besides, in the years when we began, in the years which formed us, Germany was great, wonderful, happy and free, it did not demand our attention when we painted and wrote poetry. Then came the war and as the list above shows, the Expressionists played their part in that. And in the last few years politics meant Marxism, meant Russia, assassination of all bourgeois and intellectual levels of society, assassination of all art as 'private idiocy' (Tretiakov), meant anti-heroism, dialectical rubbish, in a word, the kind of functionalism I was talking about earlier. Expressionism countered this destructive trend with inner and outer means other than political, namely with its formal absolutism which excluded all forms of chaos. Some novelists did indulge in political propaganda as well, it is true, they calmed the historical spaces regarding the longwindedness of their prose and in parliamentary democracy they found parallels for the longwindedness of their epics, but the Expressionists did not seek a world they could chat up socially, they sought an abstract world, they made art.

They were without any political instinct, there may have been a remarkable number of biological minus variants among them, moral defectives too; criminal cases, it has been proven, also occurred among them. I have no desire to whitewash this. But as against summary statements, like deserters, convicts, crooks, debased, undisciplined, phoney shares, doubtful stock-market manoeuvres, the question that has to be asked is: did not art perhaps always look like that close up? There has probably never been an art that developed in public care, not since Florence, no art which to the approving murmurs of the public fell from any acknowledged tree of knowledge. In the last few centuries art has always been anti-art, art has always been a new birth. Later, when the epochs close, when the races are dead and the kings rest in peace in their tombs, and their retinue have gone to their eternal slumbers, when the empires have come full circle and the ruins collapse between the eternal seas, then everything will look like order as if they only had to reach up to fetch down the great, gleaming wreaths lying there ready; but once it was all just as fought over, shrouded with blood, paid for with sacrifices, snatched from the underworld and snatched from the shadows. Perhaps too much time is spent nowadays on the defectives and there is too much reluctance to see that in Expressionism some works and some men certainly will survive, who with this expressive method raised themselves, their spirit, the disintegrated, tortured, shattered existence of their times up to those realms of form, in which over sunken cities and fallen empires the artist, and he alone, consecrates his age and his people to human immortality. I believe it and I am sure those I see coming will believe it . . .

POEMS

LITTLE ASTER

A drowned drayman was humped on to the slab.
Someone or other had jammed a dark light violet
    aster
between his teeth.
And as I, working
with a long knife
under the skin from the breast
cut out tongue and gums,
I must have knocked it for it slid
into the adjacent brain.
I tucked it into his breast cavity for him
between the cotton wads
as he was being sewn up again.
Drink your fill in your vase!
Rest in peace
Little aster!

HAPPY YOUTH

The mouth of a girl who had lain a long time in
    the rushes
looked so nibbled away.
The breasts broken open, the feed-pipe so full of
    holes.
Finally in a copse under the diaphragm
was discovered a nest of young rats.
One sister ratlet lay dead.
The others lived off liver and kidneys,
drank the cold blood and had
spent a happy youth here.
And short and sweet their death was too:
The whole pack were thrown into the water.
Oh! how the little snouts squeaked!

MAN AND WOMAN WALK THROUGH
THE CANCER WARD

The man:
This row here is made up of collapsed wombs.
and this row is made up of collapsed breasts.
Bed stinks by bed. The nurses change each hour.

Come, you may safely draw back this cover.
Observe, this knob of fat and fetid pus,
that was once large to some man or other
and signified passion and athomeness.

Come and observe this scar upon the breast.
Do you feel the rosary of softened knots?
Yes, touch it. The flesh is soft and feels no pain.

Here, this one bleeds as from thirty bodies.
No man on earth has so much blood.
This one here first had
a child cut out of the cancered womb.

They are left to sleep. Day and night—New ones
are told: here one sleeps one's way to health—for
Sunday visits they're made a little brighter.

Only a little nourishment is taken.
The backs are sored. You see the flies. Sometimes
the nurse washes them. As one washes benches.

Here the land is swirling up around each bed.
Flesh subsides to soil. Red heat dies off.
Sap starts to trickle. The earth is calling.

EXPRESS TRAIN

Brown as brandy. Brown as leaves. Red brown.
    Malay yellow.
Berlin-Trelleborg-Express and the east coast strands.

Flesh that went naked.
Tanned even to the mouth by the sea.
Plunged ripe, for grecian joy.
In sickle-seeking: how far off summer is!
Second last day already of the ninth month.

Stubble and last tonsil thirst within us.
Unfoldings, the blood, the tiredness,
The dahlia's proximity bemuses us.
Male brown hurls itself on female brown:

A woman's only for a one night stand.
and if all went well, perhaps for one more!
Ah! and then the being-by-yourself again!
These mutenesses! This being driven on!

A woman is something with a smell.
Ineffable! Die away! Mignonette.
There lies the South, shepherd and seas.
Joy leans on every declivity.

Female light brown falls frenzied on male dark
    brown:
Hold me! Darling, I'm falling!
My neck has grown so weary.
Oh, this sweet feverseething
last smell from the gardens.

ALASKA

Europe, that snot
on the end of a confirmand's nose
we want to go to Alaska.

Creature of sea, creature of primeval forest,
who engenders his needs out of his own belly,
who eats seals, who kills bears,
who sticks it up the women from time to time:
Man.

TRANSLATIONS

THE YOUNG HEBBEL

You fashion and shape: the pliant chisel
in a fine white hand.
I beat form out of the marble block
with my head,
my hands work for a living.

I am still so far from my real self.
But I want to become me!
Buried in my blood I bear someone,
crying for heavens and earths
he has created himself.

My mother is so poor,
you would laugh if you saw her,
we live in a narrow inlet
dug out at the end of the village.
My young life feels like a scab:
with a wound underneath
oozing blood every day.
That's what makes me so twisted.

Sleep, I don't need,
Food, only enough to keep me alive!
The struggle is relentless,
And the world is full of gaping sword points
Each hungering for my heart.
Having no other weapon I must
melt each one in my own blood.

SONGS I AND II

If we could be our primeval dawning
A piece of swamp in some warm clime
Life and death, impregnation and spawning
Could be left to our mindless slime.

Or say some sea-weed or sand thing
Something shaped by the wind, like a cone

Even a dragonfly's head or a gull's wing
Would be far too advanced and anguish prone.

Beneath contempt who loves and mocks
knows hope, despair or longing,
We are gods, though afflicted and riddled with pox
And our thoughts to god keep turning.

The dark forest dreams, the inlet's gentle seas,
Heavy, the stars bloom like snow-balls.
The panthers silently leap through the trees.
Shore everywhere. Eternally the ocean calls.

UNDERGROUND TRAIN

The softening shudders. Early flowers. As
from warm pelts it issues from the forests.
A red swarms up. The great blood rises.

Through all this spring there comes a strange woman.
The stockinged instep's there. But where it ends
is far from me. I sob at the entrance.
Half-hearted flowering, strange dampnesses.

Oh how her mouth squanders the luke-warm air!
You rose-brain, sea-blood, you twilight goddess.
You bed of earth, how coolly your hips stream
forth the passage in which you walk.

Dark: now there is life under her clothes:
All white animal, let loose and voiceless scent.

A wretched dog-brain, heavy hung with god.
My forehead wearies me. Oh that gently she'd
let loose a battery of blossom thrusts
to join the swelling and shudder and ooze.

Left so loose. So tired. I long to wander.
Bloodless the paths. Melodies from stray gardens.

Shadows and the Flood. Distant joys, a dying
away in the ocean's freeing deep azure.

ICARUS

Oh, noontide, that with hot hay reduces
my brain to meadow, flat land and shepherd,
so that I flow away, and, with my arm
in the stream, draw poppies to my temples—
O high wide-vaulted one, silently
borne on wings above the curse and woes
of creation and events
unbrain my eye.
Still through the debris of the hillside,
still through the land-carrion,
turning to dust, through the cringeing zigzag
of rock face—everywhere
the deep motherblood, the cascading
deforeheaded
sluggard
cradling.

The animal lives for the day
and has no memory in its dugs,
the slope pushes its flower in silence to the light
and is destroyed.

Only I, with sentry between blood and claw,
brain gnawed carrion with screaming
curses dying in the void, bespat with words,
made monkey of by light—
O high wide-vaulted one,
balm my eyes for an hour
with the healing early pre-eye light—
melt away the life of colours, hurl
the mud-caked caves into the ecstasy
of high rearing suns, crash of sun of suns
O eternal casting down of all suns—

II

The brain eats dust. The feet eat dust.
Were only the eye rounded and complete,
then sweet night would break in through the lids,
bracken and love.
Away from you, sweet bestial,
from your shadows, sleep and hair,
must I bestraddle my brain,
all the contortions,
the final tête-à-tête—

III

So much so on the strand, so much so in the skiff,
in the crocus coloured gown of the victim
and already round the limbs the delicate down—
you burst forth, sun, from the folds
each night new worlds into space—
O, one of these, absent-mindedly puffed this way
with its primeval furnace glow melts down **my**
      temples,
drinking up my deforeheaded blood—

THE SINGER

Germs, concept beginnings,
Broadways, azimut,
Swamp and mist born beings
Are mixed in the singer's blood.
Always in formal setting
Always towards the word
Which puts an end to forgetting
Between the 'I' and you.

A lyre neurogenous,
Pale hyperaemias,
Blood pressure blindness
Induced by caffein
There is no assessing
This steady movement to

Eternal forgetting
Between I and you.

Where formerly the singer
sang a dualistic strain
Today he is a destroyer
By means of the brain,
Hourly everything's woven
All weighty substance deployed
For the dream of the poem,
Rarely and slowly—the void.

LIFE—A BARE ILLUSION

Life—a bare illusion
Dream for children and serfs
But you of such ancient
Race at its course's conclusion.

What is there for you to do?
One more intoxication:
Or another transposition
Of world and you?

You still want a man or a wife?
Was not all there from the start,
Faith and how it departs
And the ensuing strife?

Form is the faith and the deed
Statues which hands have first touched,
They are what carry the seed.

WHOEVER IS ALONE

Whoever is alone is also in the secret,
constantly standing in the images' flow,
their begetting, their germination,
the very shadows are charged with their glow.

Swollen out with every reconstruction
fulfilled in thought, in stored-up state,
he is master of the destruction
awaiting all things that feed and mate.

Immobile he sees how for him the earth
has become another since it was born,
no more Death and no more Birth:
he meets the gaze of perfection's tranquil form.

ONE WORD

A word, a phrase, a ciphered sense
Of life perceived, of sudden meaning,
The sun stands still, the spheres in silence
All tensed towards it leaning

A word— a gleam, a fire, a soaring flight,
A cast of flame, a star across the sky—
And dark again, and endless night,
In empty space round world and 'I'.

THE LOST 'I'

The lost 'I', blasted apart by stratospheres,
victim of the ion—: gammaraylamb—
particle and field—phantom of infinities
on your grey stone of Nôtre-Dame.

The days pass on you, no dawn or darkness yield,
the years, snowless and without fruit, grip tight
the infinite, menacingly concealed—
the world as flight.

Where will you end, where make camp, the eddies
of your sphere will reach out where—gains and losses—:
a game of beasts: eternities,
you flee past their latticed bars.

TRANSLATIONS

Gaze of the beast: the stars are butcher's lights,
jungle death as Being and Creation's law.
Man, nation's, Châlon's bloody fights
swallowed down the beast's maw.

The world though to smithereens, time and space
and all mankind counted and contrived
mere functions of infinities
the myth, it lied.

Where from, where to—not night, not dawn,
No Evoë, no requiem,
you'd like to borrow some prompt, some clue—
but, ah, from whom—

Ah, when all vowed towards a common single point
and even thinkers thought of nothing but of god,
and branched out to the shepherd and the lamb now joined,
and in cleansing blood of chalice had been bathed,
and all from out that single wound did pour,
broke bread, which one and all could taste—
O distantly compelling fulfilled hour,
which once held even the lost 'I' embraced.

FRAGMENTS

Fragments,
soul's jetsam,
coagulated blood of the twentieth century—

Scars—disturbed circulation of early creation,
the historic religions of five centuries in smithereens,
science: cracks in the Parthenon,
Planck's quantum theory coagulated
with Kepler and Kierkegaard, fresh gloom—

But there were evenings, decked in the colours of
The Father Almighty, free and easy, wider ranging,
impregnable in the silence
of streaming blue,

the colour of the introverts,
then one gathered oneself,
one's hands propped on the knee,
in peasant fashion, simply,
and absorbed in a silent drink
to the harmonica of servants—

and others,
scourged by inner bundled blue-prints,
arches' pressures,
architecture's compressions
or hunting forays after love.

Crises of expression or fits of eroticism:
this is the man of today,
the interior a vacuum,
the personality's continuity
is preserved by suits,
which, if of good quality, last ten years.

The rest fragments,
half sounds,
scraps of melody from a neighbour's house,
negro spirituals
or Ave Marıas.

NOTTURNO

In the next room the dice upon the wooden table,
for neighbours a pair at the suction stage,
with a chestnut branch upon the piano
        nature joins the company—
a milieu which appeals to me.

Then the thought processes fade,
the sea-sickness which during the day
jangles the vomit nerves,
goes under in alcohol and nebulous sensations—
at last existence vanishes and the soul turns cold!

TRANSLATIONS

To recline on the waves—
naturally one can sink,
but that is a question of time—
but time—with oceans?
They came to be long long ago,
before consciousness and conception,
no one fished their monsters,
nobody suffered beyond six feet under
and that's not deep.

RESTAURANT

The gentleman over there is ordering another beer,
which suits me fine, then I don't need to reproach myself
For sinking one from time to time.
Straight off you think you are hooked,
In an American magazine I even read
Every cigarette shortens your life by 36 minutes,
I don't believe it, probably Coca Cola
Or a chewing-gum company had the article written.

A normal life, a normal death
That's not right either. A normal life also
leads to a sick death. Anyway death
has nothing to do with sickness and health,
it uses them for its own purposes.

What do you mean: death has nothing to do with sickness?
I mean it this way: many fall ill and don't die,
So there must be something else to it,
An element of doubt,
An unsafety factor,
It's not so sharply defined as all that
Doesn't have a scythe either,
Takes it all in, looks round the corner, even holds back
and is musical in a different key.

SENTENCE STRUCTURE

Everybody has heaven, love and the grave
We won't concern ourselves with these things
The culture vultures have worked them all over.
What is new, however, is the question of sentence structure
And it is pressing:
Why do we express something?

Why do we rhyme or sketch a girl
Or doodle on a hand's breadth of drawing paper
Countless plants, tree tops, walls,
the latter as fat as maggots with tortoise heads
Pulling themselves along uncannily low
In a certain order?

Overwhelmingly unanswerable!
It's not the prospect of a fee,
Many starve to death over it. No,
it is an impulse in the hand,
Remote controlled, a brain condition,
perhaps a belated saviour or totem animal,
A priapism of form at the expense of content,
It will pass,
But for today sentence structure
is primary.

TRAVEL

Do you think Zürich for instance
would be a town with more style?
Miracles galore and incense
To make your life worth while?

Or do you think Havana
White and hibiscus red
Would offer eternal manna
In your waste land for bread?

Zürich main streets, London mews,
Boulevards, lidos in plenty,
Even on Fifth Avenues,
Suddenly you feel so empty.

What use does travel serve?
Not till too late do you see:
Stay put and quietly preserve
The self-sufficient me.

CHOPIN

Not so productive in conversation,
Strong points of view were not his forte,
Strong points of view skirt the essential,
when Delacroix developed theories,
he became ill at ease, he for his part
could not defend the nocturnes.

A poor lady's man;
shadows in Nohant,
where George Sand's children
would accept none of his proposals
on how to bring them up.

A chest complaint in every sense
with haemorrhages and scar formation,
long dragged out;
A quiet death
as opposed to one with
a paroxysm of pain
or from a rifle salvo:
The grand (Erard) was moved nearer the door
and Delphine Potocka
sang for him in his last hour
a children's song.

He travelled to England with three grands:
Pleyel, Erard, Broadwood,
played at twenty guineas an evening

for quarter of an hour
at Rothchilds', Wellingtons', in Stafford House
and before innumerable Garters,
grown dark with fatigue and nearing death
he turned for home
to the Square d'Orléans.

Then he burnt his sketches
and manuscripts,
to leave no leavings, fragments, notes,
these treasonous glimpses—
said at the end:
'My efforts are perfect in proportion to that
which was within my power to attain.

Each finger was to play
in accordance with it's structure's strength,
the fourth is the weakest
(mere siamese twin to the middle finger).
When he began they lay
on E, F sharp, G sharp, B natural, C.

Whoever heard certain Preludes
of his,
be it in country houses or
on a mountain side
or through open french windows
as, for example, from a sanatorium
will find them difficult to forget.

Never composed an opera,
not one symphony,
only these tragic progressions
from artistic conviction
and with a tiny hand.

SOURCES OF THE TRANSLATIONS

PROSE

Ithaca—Ithaka, *Die weißen Blätter*, 1914 (trans. M.A.L.B.).

Brains—Gehirne, *Die weißen Blätter*, 1915 (trans. M.A.L.B.).

Address to Heinrich Mann—Rede auf Heinrich Mann, *Vossische Zeitung*, 29.3.1931 (trans. J.M.R.).

To the Literary Emigrés: A Reply—Antwort an die literarischen Emigranten, *D.A.Z.*, 25.5.1933 (trans. M.A.L.B.).

Confession of Faith in Expressionism—Bekenntnis zum Expressionismus, Deutsche Zukunft, 5.11.1933 (trans. J.M.R.).

POETRY

Little Aster—Kleine Aster, *Morgue*, 1912 (trans. R.J.K.).

Happy Youth—Schöne Jugend, *Morgue*, 1912 (trans. R.J.K.).

Man and Woman walk through the Cancer Ward— Mann und Frau gehn durch die Krebsbaracke, *Morgue*, 1912 (trans. R.J.K.).

Express Train—D-Zug, *Die Aktion*, 1912 (trans. R.J.K.).

Alaska—Alaska, *Die Aktion*, 1913 (trans. J.M.R.).

The Young Hebbel—Der junge Hebbel, *Das neue Pathos I*, 1913 (trans. J.M.R.).

Songs I and II—Gesänge I und II, *Die Aktion*, 1913 (trans. J.M.R.).

Subway Train—Untergrundbahn, *Der Sturm*, 1913 (trans. R.J.K.).

Icarus—Ikarus I-III, *Die weißen Blätter*, 1915 (trans. R.J.K.).

Cocain—Kokain, *Fleisch*, 1917 (trans. J.M.R.).

Oh Night—O Nacht, *Die Aktion*, 1916 (trans. J.M.R.).

The Singer—Der Sänger, *Spaltung*, 1925 (trans. J.M.R.).

Life, an empty illusion—Leben—niederer Wahn, *Ausgewählte Gedichte*, 1936 (trans. J.M.R.).

Whoever is alone—Wer allien ist, *Ausgewählte Gedichte*, 1936 (trans. R.J.K.).

Seeing the swords never falter—Dennoch die Schwerter halten, *Die Literatur*, 1933 (trans. J.M.R.).

One Word—Ein Wort, *Biographische Gedichte* (trans. J.M.R.).

Lost 'I'—Verlorenes Ich, *Zweiundzwanzig Gedichte*, 1943 (trans. R.J.K.).

Static Poems—Statische Gedichte, *Statische Gedichte*, 1948 (trans. J.M.R.).

Fragments—Fragmente, *Fragmente*, 1951 (trans. R.J.K.).

Notturno—Notturno, *Fragmente*, 1951 (trans. R.J.K.).

Restaurant—Restaurant, *Fragmente*, 1951 (trans. J.M.R.).

Sentence Structure—Satzbau, *Fragmente,* 1951 (trans. J.M.R.).

Poem—Gedicht, *Aprèslude,* 1955 (trans. J.M.R.).

Travel—Reisen, *Fragmente,* 1951 (trans. J.M.R.).

Chopin—Chopin, *Statische Gedichte,* 1948 (trans. R.J.K.).

Key to Translators

J.M.R.	J. M. Ritchie
M.A.L.B.	Annabel Brown
R.J.K.	R. J. Kavanagh

SELECT BIBLIOGRAPHY

WORKS

D. Wellershoff, ed., *Gesammelte Werke in acht Bänden,* Wiesbaden, 1968.

I Gedichte
II Gedichte (Anhang)
III Essays und Aufsätze
IV Reden und Vorträge
V Prosen
VI Stücke aus den Nachlaß Szenen
VII Vermischte Schriften
VIII Autobiographische Schriften

Statische Gedichte (Arche-Bücherei), Zürich, 1948.

LETTERS

Ausgewählte Briefe, Wiesbaden, 1957 (2nd ed. 1959).
Das gezeichnete Ich. Briefe aus den Jahren 1900–1956. D.T.V. Munich, 1962.
Den Traum alleine tragen...Neue Texte, Briefe und Dokumente. Wiesbaden, 1966.

BIBLIOGRAPHY

Edgar Lohner, *Gottfried Benn Bibliographie, 1912–1956,* Wiesbaden, 1958.
Edgar Lohner, ed., *Gottfried Benn (Dichter über ihre Dichtungen,* Vol. 5), München, 1969.

F. W. Wodtke, *Gottfried Benn*, Stuttgart, 1962 (2nd ed., 1970).

M. Adams, *Gottfried Benn's Critique of Substance*, Assen (1969).

E. B. Ashton, *Primal Vision,* New Directions (1958).

T. S. Eliot, *The Three Voices of Poetry,* London (1955).

R. Gray, *The German Tradition in Literature 1871–1945*, Cambridge (1965).

M. Hamburger, *Reason and Energy,* London (1957).

M. Hamburger, *From Prophecy to Exorcism,* London (1965).

M. Hamburger and C. Middleton, *Modern German Poetry 1910–1960*, London (1963).

E. Jolas, Gottfried Benn, *Transition,* **5** (1927), pp. 146–49.

V. Lange, Forms of Contemporary Poetry, *Monatshefte,* XLVI (1954), pp. 171–80.

E. Lohner, The development of Gottfried Benn's idea of expression as value, *The German Quarterly,* 1953, **26,** pp. 39–54.

H. M. Ridley, *National Socialism and Literature,* unpublished Ph.D. thesis, Cambridge (1966).

J. M. Ritchie, ed., *German Expressionist Drama,* 4 vols., London (1966–70).

J. M. Ritchie, trans., Paul Raabe, ed. *The Era of Expressionism*, London (1972).

R. Samuel and R. Hinton Thomas, *Expressionism in German Life, Literature and the Theatre 1910–1924*, Cambridge (1939).

W. Sokel, *The writer in extremis*, Expressionism in twentieth-century German literature, Stanford (1959).

D. Wellershoff, *Gottfried Benn. Phänotyp dieser Stunde*, Berlin (1958) and paperback.